Roberta Vicchi

THE MAJOR BASILICAS OF ROME

Saint Peter's
San Giovanni in Laterano
San Paolo fuori le Mura
Santa Maria Maggiore

SCALA

Contents

Introduction

Pilgrims and Jubilees

1300 is the first Holy Year in Christian history. A chronicle of the period by Giovanni Villani describes both the fervor and composure of the throngs of the faithful who came to Rome during that year from all over Europe: "... every Friday or feast day, Veronica's veil was shown in Saint Peter's for the consolation of pilgrims. A great many Christians from various far away lands made their pilgrimage to Rome, and in the city, besides the Romans, there were 200,000 pilgrims each time for the whole year long, and they stayed there without noise or riots... and I can witness to this because I was there and I saw it."

If one thinks that in that period the city of Rome had just over 150,000 inhabitants, the number indicated by our historian is truly astounding, just as astounding as the fact that the pilgrims came in such numbers despite the inevitable discomforts involved in a journey made mainly on foot and lasting many weeks, if not months, in the midst of great and unimaginable difficulties.

But Holy Year was just one more occasion in a lasting tradition common not only to Christianity but to all peoples and all religions.

In Christian culture, the idea of pilgrimage reached its greatest popularity during the Middle Ages.

All religions and cultures practice pilgrimages. Even though pilgrimage does offer social occasions such as the possibility of encountering lands, peoples, and customs different from one's own, it has always been conceived as a devotional practice, consisting in going alone or in a group to a sacred place and there performing special acts of piety to fulfill a vow or do penance.

In Christian culture, the first pilgrimages were made to Palestine as the land where Jesus and his Apostles lived. Especially after the emperor Constantine and his mother Helen had basilicas built over the tomb of Christ and on

Pages 2-3,
anonymous XVIth century artist,
View of Rome.
Mantua, Palazzo Ducale

Pisanello,
Pellegrini family coat-of-arms.
Verona, church of Sant'Anastasia

Anonymous
Catalan artist,
*Processional
banner
representing Saint
Veronica.*
Sassari, Duomo

School of
Domenico
Ghirlandaio,
*Works of Mercy:
Shelter the
Pilgrim*, detail.
Florence,
Oratory of
San Martino
dei Buonomini

Calvary, many pilgrims began to travel to the Holy Land. Before leaving they had their belt blessed, and they walked along dressed in a simple cloak, a wide-brimmed hat on their head, a knapsack over their shoulder, and a pilgrim's staff in their hand, to which they could tie a gourd to hold water. Along the way they would find monasteries and religious houses, scattered in large numbers across the countryside, to give them shelter at night. Especially during the Middle Ages thousands of pilgrims moved toward the centers of Christianity, such as Santiago de Compostela in Spain and Canterbury in England. But the most important pilgrimage site of all was always Rome, and the city of Peter's successor and of the tombs of the Apostles was equipped to receive them properly. Pilgrims to Rome were called *romei* and the roads they traveled became known as *romee*.

Besides visiting the Apostles' tombs, the pilgrims venerated also important relics like the Holy Face of Christ or Veronica's veil, which according to an ancient tradition was imprinted with the image of the Savior when she dried his sweating and suffering face with her veil on his way to Calvary.

Beginning in 1300, the pilgrimage tradition acquired the new tradition of jubilee years, taken directly from Jewish culture which, according to the Bible, every fifty years decreed a time of rest for the earth, when it would not be cultivated, when slaves and prisoners would be freed and land that had been sold be returned to its original owners.

The Jubilee in the Hebrew and Christian World

The word "jubilee" derives from the ram's horn, in Hebrew "yobel," sounded in Israel to proclaim to the people the beginning of this special year. That sound marked the beginning of an important period during which occurred events significant for society. The book of *Leviticus* speaks amply of this phenomenon. From the text emerges a picture of a society with a high moral and social sense, aimed at solidarity, the balancing out of classes and situations, at justice and love: "Seven weeks of years shall you count - seven times seven years - so that the seven cycles amount to forty-nine years. Then, on the tenth day of the seventh month let the trumpet resound; on this, the Day of Atonement, the trumpet blast shall re-echo throughout your land. This fiftieth year you shall make sacred by proclaiming liberty in the land for all its inhabitants. It shall be a jubilee for you, when every one of you shall return to his own property, every one to his own family estate. In this fiftieth year, your year of jubilee, you shall not sow, nor shall you reap the aftergrowth or pick the grapes from the untrimmed vines. Since this is the jubilee, which shall be sacred for you, you may not eat of its produce, except as taken directly from the field. In this year of jubilee, then, every one of you shall return to his own property" (*Leviticus* 25: 8-13).

The series of Christian jubilees begins on 1 January 1300. On the evening of that day, an imposing crowd of pilgrims poured into Saint Peter's, certain that a centennial year must be a time of universal pardon of sins.

Pope Boniface VIII (1295-1303), even though there was no tradition for it in the Church, on 22 February 1300 proclaimed the first Holy Year in Christian history, to be celebrated every one hundred years.

Mixed among the two million pilgrims who went to Rome that year was also Dante Alighieri (1265-1321).

The history of Holy or Jubilee Years has been subject over the centuries to various adjustments of its date. Already by 1342 Clement VI (1342-1352), from Avignon in France where the papacy had moved its seat, had changed the interval from 100 years to 50 years. Today, besides certain special occurrences, 25 years is the usual interval between jubilees.

Following tradition, the last jubilee, the 25th, was celebrated in 1975, proclaimed by Pope Paul VI (1963-1978), but the traditional series is enriched by the numerous special jubilees which the popes have called on particular occasions in the life of the Church. In the twentieth century, for instance, Pope Pius XI (1922-1939) proclaimed 1933 as a jubilee year to commemorate the nineteenth centennial of the death of Jesus Christ, and John Paul II named 1983 Jubilee Year of Redemption.

Jubilee years are marked by particular rituals, like the opening of the Holy Door or a visit to the principal churches of Rome, called the "major basilicas." On the Christmas Eve before the beginning of the jubilee year, the pope goes to the front of Saint Peter's church and with a hammer knocks symbolically three times on the door to open it. The door, through which the pilgrims will pass for an entire year to obtain the jubilee pardon, is then closed on Christmas Eve one year later.

A similar celebration takes place, presided over by three cardinals designated by the pope, in the other three major basilicas of Rome: San Giovanni in Laterano, San Paolo fuori le Mura, and Santa Maria Maggiore. The first pope to open the Holy Door in Saint Peter's was Alexander VI (1492-1503) for Holy Year 1500.

The Holy Door

Pilgrims at the Holy Door of the basilica of Santa Maria Maggiore for the Jubilee of 1975

The Holy Door, most significant symbol of Holy Year, is usually walled up and is opened only on the occasion of jubilees. The idea of a door kept closed, and opened only on these special occasions, seems to have been inspired by the ancient Christian discipline of keeping public penitents from entering the church until the entire period of their penance had passed.

The ancient ceremony of opening the door, handed down from generation to generation since 1499, is rich in symbolism and meaning. The tool used to open it is not a key, as one would imagine, but a hammer.

These blows, which according to ritual are struck by the pope, refer to a door that is hard to break open. Justice and mercy, emphasized by the Spirit of the Holy Year, can be obtained only with prayer and penance.

The words, too, that the pope pronounces while the wall blocking the door is coming down, and the congregation's response, contain the sense of this event, which officially opens the Jubilee celebrations: "This is the door of the Lord," says the pope, and the faithful add, "Through it the righteous will pass."

PORTA SANTA

Giorgio Vasari, Clement VII Opens the Holy Door for the Jubilee of 1525. Florence, Palazzo Vecchio

The Jubilee of the Year 2000

Many factors contribute to making the jubilee of the year 2000 a particularly important one. First of all, it is the first time that a Holy Year is celebrated at the same time as a new millennium.

But 2000 will open also and above all with a series of challenges for mankind: some exciting, others troubling. Think, for instance, of how things are evolving on a world-wide scale, with inevitable consequences for the economy; of the rapid development of man's potential in every field, and the danger that the great technological and scientific discoveries will increasingly relegate the individual to a position of passivity, when not of exploitation. The year 2000 of the Christian era, as it celebrates the two millennia that have passed since the birth of Christ, thus presents an occasion for reflection and one of challenge.

Pope John Paul II, in his letter preparing the faithful for the great jubilee, wrote: "Against this background, the two thousand years since the birth of Christ (ignoring the problem of the exact calculation of the year of His birth) represent an extraordinarily important Jubilee not only for Christians, but indirectly for all mankind, given the leading role that Christianity has played in these two millennia. Significantly, almost everywhere the passing of years is calculated starting from Christ's arrival in the world, which thus becomes the center of the most widely used calendar today. Is not also this a sign of the incomparable contribution made to universal history by the birth of Jesus of Nazareth?

The term 'jubilee' speaks of joy; not only of an inner joy, but of jubilation that is manifested also externally because the coming of God is also an external event, visible, audible, and tangible, as Saint John says (cf. 1 John 1:1). It is thus right that every affirmation of joy at this coming have an external manifestation. This is the indication that the Church rejoices for Salvation. It invites everyone to rejoice and it tries to create the conditions for the power of Salvation to be communicated to everyone" (*Tertio Millennio Adveniente*, 15-16).

This book which the reader is about to peruse aims at being an aid to entering into the spirit of jubilees and pilgrimages, through an ideal visit to the four major basilicas of Rome.

Thousands of pilgrims have visited them over the centuries; two of them especially, those erected over the tombs of Peter and Paul, have been the final goal of their journeys, joined by the churches of San Giovanni in Laterano and Santa Maria Maggiore.

Today little remains of the four original basilicas, but they still, despite renovations and reconstructions, are the symbol of a faith that continues to be celebrated and that leaves its mark in the work of artists of all epochs.

Like the ancient pilgrims, we shall enter through the holy doors; we shall pause in wonder before the significant monuments which adorn these sites. Going beyond words, which are always inadequate to express the richness of their contents, we shall let the marvel grow and overcome us with the beauty of the images, as prelude and preparation for a possible visit or as the memory of an experience we have already had.

This, then, is a book that aims at being not only about history and art, but a guide beyond the tangible, to the discovery of what lies at the origin of the Beautiful, which is God. Its purpose will be to help us become not only visitors or tourists, but pilgrims in search of the Absolute.

SAINT PETER'S

Peter and Rome

O ur story, which is the story of a basilica towards which millions of pilgrims have directed their steps across the centuries, begins a long time ago, in a land that the great Rome did not consider very important, even if it did send a governor there.

The figure who interests us here is a fisherman on the lake of Gennesaret in Palestine. His name is Simon.

Simon, son of Jonah, encountered Jesus of Nazareth. This encounter was overwhelming and marked the rest of his life. The Master would change his name to Peter, name him head of the twelve Apostles, and after his ascension, entrust to him the government of his Church.

Peter became an enthusiastic witness for Jesus Christ and, even with all the contradictions caused by his generous and unruly nature, dedicated to him the rest of his life. The head of the group of Apostles, he would contribute after his Master's death, resurrection, and ascension to organizing the early church in Jerusalem, then would go to Antioch and finally, around A.D. 42-44, tradition says, he reached Rome.

At the beginning of the first century, Rome was the most important city on the globe. Its territory and political and commercial influence extended throughout all the known world. However, compared to the great modern metropolises, it was little more than a village. It rose on seven hills which delimited its space, in a much smaller area than the city currently covers. One part of the city is of particular interest to us: the Vatican hill. The name Vatican in ancient times indicated the area, in part hilly and in part on the plain, outside the walls of Rome and across the Tiber river, considered too far away for habitation and used as a burial ground.

In imperial times the area, rich in parks and gardens, became the site of famous villas with splendid views, like one belonging to Agrippina, mother of Caligula (A.D. 37-41), and another belonging to the Domitians and later to Nero (54-68). In the immense garden of his mother's villa, Caligula built a great arena where he staged combats between slaves and ferocious animals. In the years around A.D. 64, the emperor Nero used that circus for cruel persecutions of the Christians, to which also the Apostles Peter and Paul fell victim, a destiny that was very probably foreshadowed by an episode in July of that same year. It is said, but it could also be legend, that Nero himself set fire to the city as a pretext for blaming the Christians for the tragedy and subjecting them to merciless persecution.

Paul was murdered by beheading, while Peter was crucified. A story, told by ancient authors like the theologian Origen (185-253/54) and Saint Jerome (c. 347-419/20), says that the Apostle, as a sign of humility, asked to be crucified upside down, as he did not feel worthy of dying in the same way Christ did. This is certainly legendary and is only one of the many fantastic stories linked with the historical figure of Peter.

Pages 10-11, Bernini's colonnade in Piazza San Pietro

Duccio di Buoninsegna, *Christ Appears on the Lake of Tiberias*, panel from the upper register of the back of the *Maestà*. Siena, Museo dell'Opera

The many episodes that tradition attributes to him during his Roman apostolate, the incredible flourishing of legends around his name, the great number of churches erected in his honor, witness to the continuing and ever increasing veneration of Christians for this martyr, and not only because Peter, the vicar of Christ, is the head of the Church, but also because among the Apostles it is difficult to find a figure who is more human or lovable than this ex-fisherman from Bethsaida by the Sea of Galilee.

For centuries it has been believed that the tomb on the Vatican hill, given a privileged position with regard to those around it and on which an imposing basilica would be erected, was the tomb of the Prince of the Apostles. However, scarce documentation and uncertain literary sources caused serious doubts to be raised over the course of the centuries. Only in recent times, and at the initiative of Pope Pius XII (1939-1958), between 1940 and 1952, were excavations carried out on the spot, resulting in unexpected finds that make it very difficult today to advance reasonable doubts about the authenticity of the tomb.

And there where Peter by dying on the cross "equalled the Passion of Christ" (Tertullian), he remains through the centuries the unmovable "rock" on which the Son of God founded his Church for all time.

From the Tomb to the Early Constantinian Basilica

Early Christian tradition refers to the existence of a small chapel built above the Apostle's simple tomb by Pope Anacletus (76-88), the second of Peter's successors, around the year 80. It immediately became a place of profound veneration on the part of the first Christians, and on these early traces three centuries later the first large basilica would be built, around A.D. 320, at the behest of the emperor Constantine (280-337) and his mother Helen.

Pope Sylvester I (314-335) took on the task of overseeing the work himself, he whom legend indicates as the one who converted Constantine after miraculously healing him of leprosy. Constantine brought to an end the persecution of the Christians, and with the edict of Milan in 313 the privileged position of the Church was recognized.

Constantine was truly a far-seeing emperor. When he came to power the general situation, particularly in the West, was not favorable to the Christians, still greatly in the minority, barely 10% of a population estimated at about 50 million, even though their faith had been recognized. The anti-Christian prejudices of the masses and the educated classes still persisted. The emperor did not lose heart, and on the foundation of the ethics and justice propounded by Christian doctrine he succeeded in unifying the empire under one faith, making also highly unpopular decisions like the one to build a

Domenico Tasselli, *The Nave and Side Aisles of the Early Constantinian Basilica*. Sacristy of Saint Peter's

Raphael, *Fire in the Borgo*, detail showing the facade of the early Constantinian basilica and the Benediction Loggia. Vatican, Raphael Stanze (Stanza dell'Incendio)

Giulio Romano and Francesco Penni, *The Donation of Constantine*, detail of the altar of Saint Peter and the apse of the early Constantinian basilica. Vatican, Raphael Stanze (Sala di Costantino)

magnificent and imposing basilica to honor the humble tomb in which Peter had been buried. Completion of the task was not easy. After a long process of filling in the site, rendered necessary by the slope of the hill in order to create enough space for the foundations, the first stone was laid.

In Raphael's Stanze in the Vatican, the fresco of *Fire in the Borgo* gives an idea of the facade of the first Saint Peter's, decorated in mosaic with the figures of Christ and the four Evangelists, in accordance with Byzantine style and taste. The facade had six large windows; at a later date,

during the papacy of Symmachus (498-514), a large rectangular court was built in front of it, called a 'paradise,' enclosed by four porticoes measuring 56 meters long and 62 meters wide. Five doors led into the basilica. The interior was a vast rectangular area, 118 meters long and 64 meters wide, divided into five nave aisles by four rows of 22 columns each.

Both inside the church and outside along the walls of the court were numerous funerary monuments honoring popes, kings, and emperors. The interior was embellished with precious marbles, mosaics, tapestries and stones of

Giulio Romano and Francesco Penni, *The Coronation of Charlemagne in Saint Peter's,* **detail. Vatican, Raphael Stanze (Stanza dell'Incendio)**

Girolamo di Benvenuto, *Gregory XI Returns to Rome from Avignon.* Siena, Società di Esecutori di Pie Disposizioni

incalculable value. Succeeding popes added to the ornate furnishings. Famous artists such as Giotto (1267-1337) and Pietro Cavallini (1240/50-?) contributed painted or mosaic decorations. Over the centuries the church's riches were subjected to theft and ruin.

Twenty-three emperors were crowned in Constantine's basilica. In 1300, the first Holy Year in history was celebrated there. The tomb of Saint Peter was in the center of the apse, surrounded by porphyry columns. By the XVth century and the papacy of Nicholas V (1447-1455), after various attempts at restoration and renovation, the church was showing the signs of wear. But above all it was seen to be inadequate to the new liturgical demands of the papacy, restored to Rome after its period of transfer to Avignon. Nicholas V initiated a project of transformation of the Late Antique and Early Christian edifice into a Renaissance basilica.

Fra Angelico, *Saint Lawrence is Consecrated Deacon by Saint Sixtus*, detail. Vatican, Chapel of Nicholas V. Saint Sixtus is represented with the facial features of Pope Nicholas V

The Pope of the First Saint Peter's Basilica: Sylvester I

Little is known about Pope Sylvester I, despite his long reign (314-335). History presents him practically as the shadow of another man, a man with a strong personality and great energy: Constantine, the first Christian emperor.
It is Constantine who fills and dominates the history of the Empire and the Church in the first half of the IVth century, to the point that even the *Liber Pontificalis*, the most extensive collection of direct information on the lives of the popes, lists and describes the emperor's constructions and donations, giving little space to the pope. But Sylvester did have the joy of seeing the Church finally free to profess its faith in public. Constantine's generous gifts

Anonymous XIIIth century artist, *The Donation of Constantine*. Rome, church of the Santi Quattro Coronati

permitted construction of great basilicas like San Giovanni in Laterano with its Baptistry, San Paolo fuori le Mura, but above all Saint Peter's on the slopes of the Vatican hill, built directly above the tomb of the Apostle. During Sylvester I's papacy, Rome began to take on the characteristics of a Christian city.
A legend tells how Constantine participated directly in the laying of the foundations for the basilica, digging the hole with his hands out of respect, and carrying on his shoulders twelve baskets of earth.
The *Liber Pontificalis* says that the emperor had a wall built around the tomb of the Apostle, enclosing it like a precious treasure. Over the tomb Constantine placed a cross of

solid gold, weighing more than 150 pounds, with the inscription: "Constantine Augustus and Helen Augusta built this royal chamber, surrounded by the Basilica shining with a similar splendor." The same source lists also other contributions from the emperor and offerings arriving in Rome from all parts of the known world to beautify and honor the Apostle's tomb and church.
At his death, Pope Sylvester I was buried in the cemetery of Priscilla on the Via Salaria.

The "New" Saint Peter's

Saint Peter's church as we see it today is the result of the laborious reconstruction of the ancient Constantinian basilica and the renovations enacted over some 120 years of continual work (1506-1626) under a succession of 18 popes and 12 illustrious architects.

The initial plan, conceived by Nicholas V, was worked out by the architects Leon Battista Alberti (1406-1472) and Bernardo Rossellino (1409-1464), but interrupted after a brief time by the pope's death. His successors for the most part promoted sporadic projects mainly at the approach of jubilee years: Pius II (1458-1464) renovated the ciborium on the altar of the Cru-

Raphael, *Portrait of Julius II*. Florence, Galleria degli Uffizi

Giorgio Vasari, *Paul III Supervises Work on Saint Peter's Basilica*. Rome, Palazzo della Cancelleria

cifixion, Sixtus IV (1471-1484) saw to its arrangement. Alexander VI (1492-1503) promoted completion of the Benediction Loggia for the year 1500.

The actual work of rebuilding the church received fresh impetus from Pope Julius II (1503-1513), who charged Donato Bramante (1444-1514) with drawing up new plans. On April 18, 1506, where the pillar called "Veronica's column" now stands, one of the four supporting the current dome of the church, the pope solemnly laid the first stone of the "new" Saint Peter's.

Julius II was a great man, energetic, decisive, and proud.

Donato Bramante, well-versed in ancient Roman building techniques, harmoniously united the architectural elements of the Pantheon and the Constantinian basilica, creating a Greek cross plan inscribed in a huge square of more than 145 meters per side and crowned by an immense dome. Two thousand workers began a tireless labor for the construction of what "in splendor and richness was to surpass every other church [in the world]" (papal bull of February 19, 1513).

The sudden death of the pope in 1513 and of Bramante the following year caused work to be suspended at the point of the four great pillars supporting the dome. Among Julius II's merits is that of having protected and encouraged great artists and architects, among them, besides Bramante, the young Raphael (1483-1520) and especially Michelangelo

XVIth century fresco showing the progress of work at Michelangelo's death, with the dome of Saint Peter's and the Benediction Loggia still unfinished. Vatican, Apartment of Julius III

(1475-1564), to whom he assigned the task of decorating the vault of the Sistine Chapel and the creation of his funerary monument. The celebrated statue of *Moses*, now in the church of San Pietro in Vincoli, was to have been an integral part of this tomb.

After Bramante's death, a succession of architects oversaw the work, above all Raphael who, modifying Bramante's plan, proposed a Latin cross, that is, with a nave longer than the transept. But Raphael's death and the damage resulting from the Sack of Rome in 1527 halted the work for a good seven years. Antonio da Sangallo (1483-1546), called by Pope Paul III (1534-1549), took up the task again for a short time.

The true turning point came only in 1547, when Michelangelo Buonarroti, at the time 72 years old, was called to direct the project.

Michelangelo, after receiving from the pope complete creative freedom, went back to the idea of a Greek cross church with a great central dome, inspired by the one over Santa Maria del Fiore in Florence. At the time of his death in 1564, work had reached the height of the drum; to complete the dome, Pope Sixtus V (1585-1590) enlisted two architects, Giacomo della Porta (1533-1602) and Domenico Fontana (1543-1607), who finished it, with the aid of 1,600 workers, in just 22 months.

Architects of the Church: Donato Bramante

Lombard school of the XVIth century, *Portrait of Bramante.* Vatican, Picture Gallery

The artistic career of Bramante (1444-1514) can be divided into two major periods. Until 1499 he worked in Lombardy, and in particular in Milan; then, for the remaining fifteen years of his life he stayed in Rome. His early activity, marked by research based on the work of the great XVth century artists like Brunelleschi and Alberti, laid the premises for the course Renaissance architecture would take after him.

The culmination of this development can be seen in the plans for the church of Santa Maria delle Grazie in Milan. The ingenious solutions created here foreshadow what would be the great project of his maturity: Saint Peter's in Rome. Julius II was able to take full advantage of Bramante's skill, naming him general supervisor of all the papal building projects.

Bramante was responsible for two fundamental enterprises: a connector between the Vatican buildings and the villa built for Pope Innocent VIII (1484-1492) on the top of the Vatican hill, and above all the new Basilica of Saint Peter's, commenced on 18 April 1506. Bramante did not see the completion of either of these projects, which in fact were subjected to radical transformation, but the ingenious and magnificent solutions he proposed provided the base for the inspirations and orientations of High Renaissance architecture. Other artists received and continued his heritage. Among many, noteworthy are Baldassare Peruzzi (1481-1536), Antonio da Sangallo the younger (1483-1546), and Jacopo Sansovino (1486-1570).

The Artist: Michelangelo Buonarroti

Domenico Cresti, called Passignano, *Michelangelo Presents the Model of Saint Peter's to the Pope,* detail. Florence, Casa Buonarroti

Painter, sculptor, architect, man of letters, already during his lifetime Michelangelo (1475-1564) was considered the supreme genius of Renaissance art, equal and superior to the ancients. Some facts of his life help us to understand aspects of his art. Born in Tuscany, he was and always remained a son of the land of his birth, continuing the monumental Tuscan tradition of Giotto and Masaccio. Tuscan, too, was his way of being passionate, daring, and proud at the same time that he was reserved and sincere. The loss of his mother at six years of age can explain the type of Madonnas lacking in tenderness that he painted in his early years. An important role in Michelangelo's life was played by his protectors, ideal fathers severe like Pope Julius II or benevolent like Lorenzo de' Medici. Only two of his friends had a significant influence on him: Tommaso Cavalieri and Patrizio Romano. Vittoria Colonna, a member of one of the leading families of the Italian aristocracy, was his spiritual guide in his late religious conversion.

The enormous success of his art created two opposing images among his contemporaries: his friends and admirers turned him into a myth, while his adversaries and critics spread the idea of a misanthrope, gloomy, haughty, miserly, and even heretical. When in 1863 his poems and in 1875 his letters were published in their correct form, the picture emerged of a noble and generous nature.

The artist would have liked to die or at least to be buried in Florence. He died instead in Rome, on 18 February 1564, and was buried the next day in the church of Santi Apostoli there. An inventory of the property left at his death indicates a fairly modest estate. His nephew Leonardo, respecting his uncle's desire, had his body stolen and transported secretly to Florence, where it arrived on 10 March. A funeral was celebrated in the church of Santa Croce, and his mortal remains now lie in the tomb designed for him by Vasari.

Completion of the Basilica

Sixtus V is the pope who more than any other contributed to changing the urban plan of Rome. In the brief five years of his papacy, with building projects rapidly drawn up and just as rapidly carried out, the pope gave the city a prophetically new face, the first European model of a modern metropolis. Reorganization of the roads system, reconstruction of the Lateran Palace, construction of the Apostolic Palace in the Vatican and a new home for the Apostolic Library, are just a part of the building activity that attracted great praise but also heavy criticism from his contemporaries and from modern historians. Many of his undertakings, in fact, involved the demolition of important structures both from the historical and the artistic points of view.

A pope so active and swift to decide could not but intervene also in the work on the new basilica, commenced in 1451 under Pope Ni-

Cesare Nebbia and Giovanni Guerra, Transport of the Obelisk. Vatican Library, Salone Sistino

Cesare Nebbia, The Coronation of Sixtus V on the Steps of Saint Peter's. Vatican Library, Salone Sistino

cholas V and not yet brought to a conclusion. Sixtus V charged the architects Giacomo della Porta and Domenico Fontana with carrying out Michelangelo's plans for the dome, which was finished on 21 June 1590, little more than two months before his death on 27 August from malaria. The dome, says a note of the announcements in Rome of 1590, was erected "to the perpetual glory of His Blessedness and the discomfiture of his predecessors."

In 1586, on 10 September, Pope Sixtus V installed the obelisk in Saint Peter's Square, along with the dome one of the best known symbols of Saint Peter's.

Under Paul V (1605-1621) construction of the basilica was finished. In many ways Paul V can be considered the true father of the church as it stands now. At the time of his election, discussion as to whether the church should represent a Greek cross, that is, be on a central plan with arms of equal length, as originally designed by Bramante, or a Latin cross, which called for a longer nave, had not yet been resolved. It seems that two reasons led the pope to choose the second solution: first, the idea of using optimally all the sacred space of the first Constantinian basilica which was on a longitudinal plan, and second, liturgical demands. In fact, for too many years by that point the papal celebrations had taken place in an area not adequate to the purpose and next to open construction sites, separated by just a temporary wall which Pope Paul III (1534-1549) had built to reserve a minimum of respect for the sacred space.

The architect who carried out the pope's decisions was Carlo Maderno (1556-1629); he brought the church to its current size, completing it with its solemn, imposing facade. Paul V died on 28 June 1621 and was buried in his magnificent chapel in Santa Maria Maggiore.

One work alone is sufficient to lend prestige to the name of Carlo Maderno: the facade of Saint Peter's basilica. In that period, when architecture was not studied at the university but in workshops alongside the great masters, Maderno's artistic training could take place in only one way. Called to Rome from his birthplace in the Ticino area of Switzerland by his uncle, the no less famous Domenico Fontana, the young Carlo began truly "at the bottom," working as stone cutter and stucco decorator.

His spirit of observation and the example of a great teacher, along with his clearly evident personal abilities, made him a master himself, in fact a key personality in the process of architectural renewal, to the point of attracting Pope Paul V's attention to his plans for the completion of Saint Peter's.

From 1607 to 1612, Maderno gave form to his concept, which deviated from both Bramante's early plan and Michelangelo's. The architect clearly had to make considerable compromises in order to respect at least in part the intentions of the masters who preceded him, and this led to solutions which in some cases are not optimal. The current facade, for example, although low and wide, still does not allow Michelangelo's dome to emerge with its original impression of height.

Maderno, in any case, and his architectural solutions deserve credit for having articulated the imposing bulk of the church, respecting the space in front of it and laying the premise for the urban design enacted later by Bernini (1598-1680) with the construction of the immense Saint Peter's square, bounded by his celebrated colonnade.

By this point, Saint Peter's basilica lacked very little in order to appear in all the majesty that we see today. Two popes would finish it: Urban VIII (1623-1644) and Alexander VII (1655-1667). Many important chapters in the Church's history felt the stimulus of Urban VIII. An example is his commitment to enacting the directives of the Council of Trent and his particular impulse toward missionary activity. But his pastoral and political actions were shadowed also by numerous factors, such as the increase in nepotism which gave to family and friends positions for which they were often not qualified.

**Barberini
manufacture of the
XVIIth century,
*Urban VIII
Consecrates
Saint Peter's
Basilica*. Vatican,
Galleria degli
Arazzi**

Giovanni Paolo Pannini, *Charles III at Saint Peter's.* **Naples, Museo Nazionale di Capodimonte**

Loving splendor, a refined connoisseur of art and generous patron of artists, Urban worked to make Rome, the seat of the papacy, appear as truly the "caput mundi." Among other endeavors, he gave particular attention to decorating Saint Peter's basilica, which he consecrated on 18 November 1626.

He found in Gian Lorenzo Bernini, already an esteemed artist despite his young age, an attentive and valuable collaborator as well as the executor of his projects, which he himself oversaw with great zeal.

Bernini was given the commission to erect the celebrated splendid canopy, or "*baldacchino*," over the papal altar, as well as to design Urban's tomb in the apse of the church, rightly considered a masterpiece and the prototype of XVIIth century funerary art. The pope was laid to rest here after his death on 29 July 1644. Bernini's celebrated bronze bust of Urban VIII, noted for its expressive effect, reveals the signs of the esteem uniting the greatest artist of the Roman Baroque and the pope who discovered him and recognized his worth.

But another pope was yet to come who, besides holding Bernini in esteem as had Urban VIII, commissioned from him the design of what is now Saint Peter's Square with its two open colonnades like arms embracing it. This pope was Alexander VII, the last of the great ideal fathers of Saint Peter's Basilica.

The Popes of the Basilica: Alexander VII

Gian Lorenzo Bernini, *Tomb of Alexander VII*. Rome, Saint Peter's

Medallion from the papacy of Alexander VII with Bernini's design for Piazza San Pietro. Vatican Library

Borromini (1599-1667) and Pietro da Cortona (1596-1669, but above all Gian Lorenzo Bernini, who designed for him the altar of the Throne of Saint Peter and the most famous colonnade in the world in the square outside. It took almost a year of lively debate to overcome objections and difficulties, but in the end it was the pope himself who chose, from among the many presented, the model of what would become the square as we see it today.

Pope Alexander VII, with the precision for which he is known, on 20 May 1657 wrote in his diary: "Cavalier Bernino showed the plans and elevation of the porch of Saint Peter's and we shall finish it like this."

Gian Lorenzo Bernini, who had already designed Urban VIII's tomb, built also the funerary monument for Alexander VII, who died on 22 May 1667, when construction of the colonnade was practically complete.

A s confirmation of the idea that Pope Alexander VII (1655-1667) was a methodical and precise man devoted to writing down everything that became the object of his desires, he left a diary. Besides personal comments, the pope gave us in this manuscript lists of building projects for the city of Rome that, like for his predecessor Urban VIII, had to present itself significantly as the "civitas" par excellence of the Catholic world. This commitment, which shows the pope to have been not only the promoter but also the instigator of ideas and solutions, sometimes technical ones, received the support of prestigious artists like Francesco

The Artist: Gian Lorenzo Bernini

Bernini (1598-1680), who for a half century was a significant presence in Roman artistic culture, is the most complex genius of Baroque art. Among XVIIth century masters, he is the one who contributed the most quantitatively to changing the face of the city of Rome, making Saint Peter's Square its most representative urban space.

His true role was not that of revolutionary, but of a mediator between various tensions. Saint Peter's is the site of Bernini's most daring architectural and sculptural creations.

Gian Lorenzo Bernini, *Self-Portrait.* **Florence, Galleria degli Uffizi**

His art was at the service of seven popes, from Paul V to Innocent XI (1676-1689). The two popes who most utilized his talents were Urban VIII, who commissioned the tomb on which Bernini worked for almost twenty years, and Alexander VII, who entrusted to him the plan for the square in front of the church. The problems he had to face were manifold: above all to conserve the existing structures and to permit a greater visibility of the Apostolic Palaces, and also the need to correct significant errors in the alignment of the church, its facade, and the obelisk. The result is there for all to see: a wide sweep of space which in the lively dynamics of its relationships diminishes the excessive width of the facade and communicates directly the metaphor of welcoming open arms.

Bernini showed his ability to unite profoundly art with the ideal of faith, of which his great architectural works become the instrument. The master's artistic activity was linked not only with the design of the colonnade but also with the embellishment of the basilica's interior. A chronicle written in 1710 tells that "Bernini, struck by paralysis, lost the use of his arm, and joking about his own infirmity, recognized that it was fair to give his arm and hand a little rest after so much work. Then he never got better, and in November of that year he died." It was 1680.

The Church Today

The majestic
front of the
facade of the
basilica, built by
Carlo Maderno
between 1607
and 1614

On facing page,
detail of Bernini's
colonnade in
Piazza San Pietro

From the time work first commenced on the new basilica under Nicholas V, to the completion of its construction, 168 years had to pass and 26 popes to sit on the Throne of Peter. Thousands of workers contributed to its construction, during certain periods also day and night. Papal records show that just for the construction of the four piers supporting the great dome 70,653 ducats were spent, a truly e-normous sum for that time. The greatest architects of the Renaissance contributed to its conception and realization. It was inaugurated by Paul V on 12 April 1615.

From the door to the apse, the basilica measures 186.86 meters long and 140 meters wide, making it still today the largest church in the world. The obelisk in the square had been erected already on 10 September 1586. A few more years still would pass before Gian Lorenzo Bernini could design and build his famous colonnade.

Today the basilica covers a surface of 25,616 sq. meters. It has 44 altars and 11 domes, 778 columns, 395 statues, and 135 between images and mosaics.

After narrating the history of the major milestones along the path from the humble tomb of Saint Peter to the construction of the great basilica, like pilgrims we enter the space of Saint Peter's Square, welcomed by the wide arms of its colonnade.

It is not this publication's intention to lead the reader to discover the basilica in detail. Instead, we shall let ourselves be struck by its

Pages 28-33,
Views of the
basilica showing
the square and
Vatican Palaces

Michelangelo's dome with, in the foreground, the statues on the entablature of the colonnade

On facing page, architectural details of the basilica

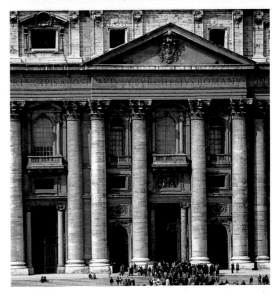

An evocative view of the obelisk with the colonnade and Apostolic Palace, the pope's current headquarters

On facing page, the apse designed by Michelangelo

most outstanding aspects, which will become for us as well signs of a faith that over the centuries has acted as the unifying agent in the construction of the church itself.

Saint Peter's Square welcomes us not only with its sweeping colonnade but also with the imposing obelisk set in its center.

The obelisk came originally from Heliopolis in Egypt, and had stood next to old Saint Peter's in the area of Nero's circus. It was moved under the papacy of Sixtus V in 1586.

The complex operation, directed by the architect Domenico Fontana, lasted four months and employed 907 men, 75 horses, and 40 winches.

It was also necessary to demolish some houses next to the church. The great red granite monolith rests on the backs of four bronze lions by the sculptor Prospero Antichi, on a base of 8.5 meters. It is 25.31 meters tall and is the only one in Rome without hieroglyphic inscriptions. It is also a solar timepiece: the white marble discs in the square are inscribed with a sun-dial and the points of the compass, the work in 1817 of the astronomer L.F. Gilij, who used the obelisk as a gnomon.

The atrium of
Saint Peter's

On facing page,
stucco decoration
on the vault of
the atrium

Antonio Averulino,
called Filarete,
bronze door and
(left) detail of
*Saint Peter Giving
the Keys to the
Kneeling Pope
Eugene IV*

The Atrium of Saint Peter's and Its Five Doors

In ancient basilicas the atrium had not only a functional aspect, but also a liturgical meaning, as it was the area fostering the passage from daily life, marked by tasks and commitments, to that of prayer, marked by contemplation.

Saint Peter's atrium is not exempt from this significance. Its characterizing elements are the five doors that lead the visitor into the church, recalling the five nave aisles of old Saint Peter's.

The central entrance is the oldest; the one called the Holy Door is opened only for Jubilee Years, and three are very recent, having been installed in the twentieth century after an international competition and decorated by bronze doors.

The portal of the central door is the work of the Tuscan artist Antonio Averulino

two great panels represent the heroic deaths of Bible characters and saints. Following an ancient tradition, the door is opened on the day of the funeral of the pope to allow passage of the funeral cortege into the basilica.

The second, the work of Venanzo Crocetti (1913-?), is called the Door of the Sacraments because of the decorations on its bronze plaques referring to the sacraments.

The artists Nagni and Monteleone created the Door of Good and Evil, which was consecrated on 26 September 1977 for Pope Paul VI's eightieth birthday. The iconography sets up a dialectic in its two panels between Good and Evil, using episodes from sacred mythology and from the history of the faith. The entire door is pervaded by a dramatic expressivity that corrodes the forms to the point of shaping them with violence.

Giacomo Manzù, *Door of Death*, detail

called Filarete (1400-1469), who finished it in 1445, a date that appears on the panels. Its elegant and rich decoration is a hymn to Christ, the Virgin Mary, and the Apostles Peter and Paul. The iconographical program emphasizes the desire to affirm forcefully the ecumenical, political, and religious primacy of the Church of Rome, ratified by the sacrifice of the Apostles and martyrs. This clearly didactic intent is justified by the necessity of Pope Eugene IV (1431-1447) to underline his commitment to resolving the dissension with the Eastern Church. The first door on the left was commissioned by Pope John XXIII (1958-1963) from his fellow townsman the artist Giacomo Manzù (1908-1991). It is called the Door of Death because its

The Interior of the Church

Giovanni Paolo Pannini, *Interior of Saint Peter's.* **Paris, Louvre; below, interior of the dome decorated with late XVIth century mosaics**

Entering Saint Peter's, one's first reaction is astonishment. The visitor is practically overwhelmed by the grandiose nature of the church, but the sensation lasts only an instant, because little by little the immensity surrounding him leads him to feel part of a

View of the nave,
from the dome

Pages 42-43,
interior of the
basilica

larger reality and to enter thus into a dimension of pure contemplation.

The edifice, the fruit of the sublime work of numerous artists, testifies to the perennial faith of the Church founded on Christ and narrates the glory, power, strength and beauty of God present in the temple that welcomes those who believe in him.

The Apostle Peter, the first pope, was an eye-witness to God made man. His bronze statue is the goal of millions of pilgrims who come from every part of the world to venerate the saint and pray at his tomb. The statue's right foot is worn away by the kisses of the faithful, who still today repeat this ancient gesture of devotion.

Attributed to Arnolfo di Cambio (1245-1302), the statue represents Peter seated in the act of blessing, while he holds in his hand the keys symbolizing the power granted him by Jesus Christ to govern the Church.

Every year on the feast of Saint Peter, 29 June, the statue is dressed in sacred vestments and crowned with the papal triple crown, the traditional liturgical headdress for popes, which Paul VI (1963-1978) gave up as a visual gesture of the idea that the papacy should be lived not as power but as service to the Church.

The gaze of the visitor entering Saint Peter's inevitably is attracted to the center of the church, the site of the altar of the Confession with its celebrated *baldacchino*.

Michelangelo's Pietà

However, before moving to the space under the dome, one should stop for a moment in front of the first chapel on the right.

A statue, which everyone will certainly recognize, attracts the eye. It is the first of Michelangelo's four versions of the *Pietà*, the only one he finished and the only work he signed.

At the moment of this work's creation, Michelangelo was just 24 years old. It seems that when it was shown for the first time, the sculpture was attributed by some viewers to another artist and not this young unknown sculptor. The story is told that Michelangelo hid in the church at night after it was closed and carved his name into the strap crossing the Virgin's bodice.

The sculpture's originality is immediately evident. Often when representing the Virgin with her dead Son in her arms, artists have shown her as desperate and broken in her grief. Michelangelo has instead given us a different vision of human grief: the celestial face of the mother holding the lifeless body of Christ radiates an unparallelled sweetness, a serene and dignified acceptance of pain. It is said that Michelangelo, responding to criticism that he had made Mary too young when in reality she should have been at least 45-50 years old, said that he had done it on purpose, as the action of time could not leave its mark on the face of the Virgin, symbol of eternal youth.

The marble group is today protected by bullet-proof glass, since in 1972 a deranged man struck it with a hammer, damaging part of the nose and hand of the Virgin.

Michelangelo,
Pietà. Chapel
of the Pietà

The Sacellum of the Tomb of Peter

The ideal center of Saint Peter's Basilica, the spot toward which the feet of millions of pilgrims have been directed, is the tomb of the Apostle. On this simple sepulchre, reached by two wide semicircular ramps, around which 99 oil lamps burn, two basilicas have been raised, precious treasure chests holding the body of the one to whom Christ entrusted his Church: *"Tu es Petrus et super hanc petram aedificabo ecclesiam meam et tibi dabo claves regni caelorum"* ("You are Peter, and upon this rock I will build my church... I will give to you the keys to the kingdom of heaven" (*Matthew* 16:18-19). These words, inscribed in the circular band at the base of the great dome, testify to the Savior's will to give visible continuity to his presence in the community of the faithful through the figure of Peter and his successors. At the center of the sacellum is a richly decorated niche and a silver urn containing the "pallia," white lambswool stoles which the pope gives to patriarchs and metropolitan archbishops as a symbol of Christ the Good Shepherd, represented by the bishops in their ecclesial communities.

The perennially-burning lamps illuminating the tomb of Saint Peter and the statue of *Pius VI Praying*, a work by Canova finished by Adamo Tadolini.

The niche containing the pallia under the Confessio

The Altar of the Confession: Bernini's Baldacchino

On a vertical axis with Peter's tomb, the sign of the Apostle's martyrdom and thus "confession" of his faith, which he professed to the point of giving his life, stands the altar where the pope normally celebrates the solemn liturgies.

The altar, made of a block of white marble, was consecrated by Pope Clement VIII (1592-1605). Its direct spatial relationship with Peter's tomb highlights the continuity of every liturgical celebration with the Apostle and through him with Christ.

On this altar Bernini, still a young man, in ten years of long and arduous labor constructed the celebrated *baldacchino* commissioned by Urban VIII and rightly considered one of the symbols of Saint Peter's and one of the most important works of Baroque art.

To realize this imposing bronze monument measuring 29 meters from its base to the top of the cross, the pope had to spend one tenth of the Church's income and melt the bronze covering of the beams on the porch of the Pantheon. This endeavor was not to the liking of the Roman people, who coined a well-known Latin saying, denouncing the pope, member of the Barberini family, as more barbarous than the barbarians: *"quod non fecerunt barberi, fecerunt Barberini."* The work was concluded in 1633 and is the largest known art work in bronze.

The great canopy is supported by four twisted columns decorated by branches of olive and laurel spiralling toward the top, with garlands so light that they seem to sway with the wind.

Bernini's inspiration for the columns was provided by the eight columns which he himself had moved to the balconies of the relics and that had earlier decorated the high altar of old Saint Peter's. It seems that these columns came from Greece, or even from Solomon's Temple in Jerusalem.

The *baldacchino*, which covers the altar and Peter's tomb, develops the idea of the tent that covers, protects, and exalts, but it also is an explicit reference to the prologue to the Gospel of Saint John where the Word of God was made flesh and dwelt among us (1:14).

The Balconies of the Relics

In the great piers supporting the dome of Saint Peter's, Pope Urban VIII had four niches created, covered by a canopy and opening onto a balcony. Each of these conserves an important relic of the Passion of Christ. Underneath, in niches at the bottom of the piers, are four statues of

On facing page, the monumental bronze *Baldacchino* by Bernini

Gian Lorenzo Bernini, *Saint Longinus*

saints (Veronica, Helen, Longinus, and the Apostle Andrew) holding the emblem of the precious relics which are preserved above them.

Bernini himself planned and realized this project, sculpting also the statue of *Saint Longinus*, clearly the most beautiful of the four, which were done by different artists. Longinus is the soldier who, according to Saint John the Evangelist (John 19:34) pierced Christ's side with a lance; later, after his conversion, he too died a martyr.

What was according to tradition Longinus' lance was given to Pope Innocent VIII (1484-1492) by the sultan Bajazet, son of Mohammed I, in 1492.

The lance, together with Veronica's veil and a relic of the True Cross, which according to an ancient tradition was found by Saint Helen, the mother of Constantine, in Jerusalem near Calvary, was exhibited to the veneration of pilgrims especially during Holy Years.

The German Chapel of the "New Grottoes"

On facing page: Gian Lorenzo Bernini, *Cathedra of Saint Peter*, and, below, detail of the statue of *Saint Augustine*

The Vatican Grottoes

A short flight of stairs leads from the pillar of *Saint Longinus* to the Vatican Grottoes, a vast underground area created between the papacies of Gregory XIII (1572-1585) and Clement VIII. The Grottoes originated at the time of construction of the new Saint Peter's. The floor of the church was raised some two meters above the level of the Constantinian basilica, and the space between them was used to house the funerary monuments, sculptures, and mosaics originally in the older church.

The area is divided principally into two parts: one with three aisles and a cross vault called the "Old Grottoes," in which numerous popes' tombs were placed, and a semicircular area around Peter's tomb, called the "New Grottoes," from which radiate side chapels holding the funerary monuments of the most recent popes. With special permission, it is possible to go down from the Vatican Grottoes to the pre-Constantine necropolis (II-III century A.D.).

The altar of the Cathedra

In the apse of the basilica stands an altar, with above it the *Cathedra of Saint Peter*, created by Bernini between 1658 and 1666.

The seats of bishops, and in particular that of the pope, are normally called *cathedrae* to underline the duty to teach which is integral to the tasks of bishops and in particular of the pope.

A legend tells that in this magnificent shell is inserted the seat where Peter, aging and weary, would sit while he taught the first Christians. In reality it is a wooden throne decorated with finely incised ivory panels, given to the pope by the German emperor Charles the Bald (823-877) after his coronation in Rome in 875.

This work realized in bronze by Bernini is thus like a great reliquary in the shape of a throne, which the artist conceives as held up by four Doctors of the Church, two representing the Eastern Church: Athanasius and John Chrysostom, and two for the Western Church, Ambrose and Augustine.

Since antiquity the Church has called doctors those who contributed in a decisive way to spreading the message of the Revelation.

Bernini places them at the foot of the papal throne as though supporting it, to emphasize their contribution to the authoritative teaching of the pope. The golden rays, with the dove of the Holy Spirit in the center, indicate that the pope in his role as teacher to all the Church receives illumination and inspiration from God himself.

In this work by Bernini, architecture and sculpture, gold, glass, marble and bronze all meld together to create an interplay of light and shadow, giving life to a complex and highly original composition, the true expressive culmination of Baroque art.

Imperial throne of Charles the Bald, traditionally held to be the episcopal throne of Peter

The Papal Tombs

One hundred forty-seven popes are buried in Saint Peter's basilica. It is easy to understand the desire of many successors of the Prince of Apostles to be buried near where the first pope had witnessed to his faith and now lay in his tomb. Some popes still during their lifetimes called leading artists to create their funerary monuments. It is well known that Julius II gave this task to Michelangelo, who, however, for various reasons never succeeded in finishing the work, causing him profound artistic and psychological turmoil.

The popes' funerary monuments, scattered along the nave aisles or placed in the Grottoes, can easily recount not only the history of the papacy but also that of art, from the medieval and Renaissance monuments all the way to our day. The excessiveness of the Baroque gives way to the essentiality of modern art; carved marble alternates with cast bronze. Each of these monuments, although inevitably in a celebratory style, in the features of the figures represented and the allegorical symbols which often surround them narrates a chapter of the story of the Church of Rome. Enlarging the scope of this story beyond that of just the papacy are the monuments raised to saints and sovereigns.

In Saint Peter's is truly represented all the history of the Church, conceived as God's people, in which each one with his gifts and characteristics contributes to the growth of the community as a whole.

Monument to Paul III. Paul is the pope who called the Council of Trent in 1545 and entrusted to Michelangelo supervision of the work of constructing the new Saint Peter's. Michelangelo wrote of him: "The pope has shown only kindness to me." Michelangelo's style seems to have inspired Guglielmo della Porta (c. 1490-1577), creator of this imposing monument.

Michelangelesque are the figures of the pope and the elderly woman near the bottom, to the viewer's right, with features similar to those of the Cumaean Sibyl painted by the great artist on the Sistine Chapel ceiling. Some historians have claimed to see in this statue the physiognomy of Giovannella Caetani, the mother of Paul III. The other statue at the bottom seems to portray Giulia, the pope's beautiful sister. In any case, the two statues represent the allegories of *Prudence* and *Justice*.

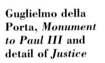

Guglielmo della Porta, *Monument to Paul III* and detail of *Justice*

Monument to Urban VIII. To the right of the *Cathedra* of Saint Peter is the funerary monument raised by Bernini to Pope Urban VIII, which can be considered the Baroque prototype for works of this type.

The figure of the pope, who was the artist's first great protector, is real-

ized in bronze gilt. Next to the sarcophagus, two female figures in white Carrara marble are allegories of *Charity* and *Justice*. Atop the sarcophagus Death, shown as a winged skeleton, holds a roll of parchment on which are inscribed the pope's name and family of origin.

Bernini worked some twenty years to make this monument, from 1627 to 1647, finishing it three years after Urban's death.

The Chapels in Saint Peter's Basilica

In ancient Early Christian basilicas, there was only one altar because there is only one Christ, symbolized by the altar, and only one Eucharist celebrated by the bishop and priests together. Over the centuries, liturgical dispositions gave priests the possibility of celebrating alone for special intentions, and the churches responded by adding altars and chapels along the side aisles.

In the XIIth century, the Vatican basilica alone had more than thirty altars.

The chapels and numerous altars in Saint Peter's respond to those exigencies of the liturgy that now, after reform, has been restored to its original meaning. Above the altars are images like the beautiful bas-relief of Pope Leo the Great (440-461), shown in the moment of his opposition to Attila, or the tender image called the "Madonna of the Column," venerated already in the ancient basilica of Constantine. Many of these images are faithful reproductions in mosaic of famous and precious works whose originals, for evident reasons of conservation and security, are kept in the museums, such as Raphael's celebrated *Transfiguration*, now in the Vatican picture gallery.

Alessandro Algardi, *Leo the Great Meets Attila*. Chapel of the Column

The Chapel of the Blessed Sacrament. An elegant iron grate with stucco gilt decoration, the work (1629/30) of Francesco Borromini, leads to what was originally destined to be a sacristy and in the early years of the XVIIth century became the Chapel of the Blessed Sacrament.

The story of the chapel and its decoration is quite complex; it was taken up by various artists following preparatory drawings by Pietro da Cortona (1596-1669), who painted the *Trinity* which now hangs above the central altar. Above the altar on the right is a mosaic representing *The Ectasy of Saint Francis*, copy of a work by

Domenichino in the church of Santa Maria della Concezione in Rome. Gian Lorenzo Bernini is the author of the tabernacle realized in 1674 and conceived as a small central plan *tempietto*, clearly inspired by the one Bramante designed for San Pietro in Montorio; he also oversaw the restoration of the floor and the chapel rail.

To this ideal place, important as an artistic composition but above all for the function to which it is destined, we now direct the steps of those who by this point are at the end of their visit to Saint Peter's. Here one truly cannot be just a tourist, but is also a pilgrim.

This spot is reserved exclusively to prayer and reflection. The Host is daily exposed here, and the wonder and awe that the great art works have aroused in us are now called to tranform themselves in the believer into an act of faith in him who, present in the Eucharist, is the central impulse from which every inspiration arises. But art, daughter of beauty, can be enjoyed also by those who profess other faiths. Also for them this chapel, purposely kept separate from the clamoring voices of daily life, can be the occasion for reflection on what the great art works have been able to impart to their souls.

SAN GIOVANNI IN LATERANO

Between History and Legend

San Giovanni in Laterano is the cathedral of Rome, and as such is the privileged seat of papal authority, symbolically represented by the bishop's cathedra. As the pope's cathedral it is ideally the first of the world's churches, or, as an ancient saying goes, "the mother of all churches."

Its story is complex, as complex as the tracing of all the milestones on a journey that goes from the emperor Constantine (280-337) to the church as we see it today, where very little is left of the early structure. The origins of this sa-

Cristoforo Roncalli, called Pomarancio, *Pope Sylvester Baptizes Constantine*. Left transept

Pages 62-63, interior of San Giovanni in Laterano

cred edifice are rooted in legend. The best known among the many legends which sprang up in the Middle Ages tells that the emperor Constantine was suffering from leprosy when Peter and Paul appeared to him in a dream and promised him he would get well if he were baptized. The pope at that time was Sylvester I (314-335), who had fled Rome for fear of persecution and lived in hiding among the forests of

Mount Soracte. Reassured by the emperor, he agreed to return to Rome and baptize Constantine. Healed of his leprosy, Constantine as a sign of gratitude built the basilica of San Giovanni.

The story is unlikely also because, if Constantine was baptized, and this has not been historically proven, it would have happened only in the last years of the emperor's life. In any case, it would be opportune, for the sake of clarity, to proceed in an orderly fashion.

The basilica of San Giovanni is often called simply "the Lateran." The name probably derives from the ancient Roman family of the Laterani, who during the First Empire lived in a still unspecified part of the current area of Rome called Laterano.

Tacitus, in his *Annals*, reports that a certain member of that family, Plautius Lateranus, after organizing a plot against Nero, was discovered and killed, and his goods confiscated. The area of city where the Laterani property was located became known as the Laterano.

Historians disagree on the origins of this Early Christian church and on the archaeological finds brought to light in numerous excavation campaigns. Some say that in the IVth century there existed on the site of the current church a *domus ecclesia*, a place where Christians gathered together to pray, created in the house of Fausta, Constantine's wife. Here the church was erected by the emperor sometime between 310 and 315. Others say that the *domus ecclesia* was built on the ruins of the houses belonging to the Laterani, thus a few hundred meters away from the spot where the church now stands, under which have been

found the remains of a building from the end of the IIIrd century. This building later became the headquarters of the imperial private guard; the emperor demolished it in order to build there the Early Christian basilica dedicated to the Savior and later given the names also of Saints John the Baptist and John the Evangelist during the papacy of Gregory I (590-604). Of these two hypotheses, the second appears more probable, even though some historians are not convinced.

The ancient structure was very similar in plan

to the current one, and the perimeter of the ancient walls coincides more or less with those of the church today. The nave and four aisles were separated by splendid marble columns with Corinthian capitals; the transept was limited to the three central aisles, while the two outer aisles were shorter than the others and terminated in two square areas protruding a few meters from the side walls.

Next to the church were buildings which for about 1000 years housed not only the residence of the pope but also the papal curia. The basilica and buildings were the seat of five ecumenical councils, called Lateran councils because of their site. With the transfer of the Holy See to Avignon (1304), the architectural complex of the Lateran began a long period of decline, which lasted even after the popes returned to Rome in 1378. After the so-called "Avignon exile" the popes preferred to live in the Vatican.

Only under Pope Sixtus V (1585-1590), when the church and palaces were in a shocking state of disrepair, was the decision made to subject the complex to radical restoration.

Today the church is still the cathedral of Rome, the ideal seat of the authority of the pope, of which the cathedra is the symbol. It may not house efficacious and exceptional relics like the tombs of Saint Peter and Saint Paul, but its ideal attraction is stronger even than relics because it is linked to the message that "made all things new" (*Revelation* 21:5), that of the Son of God made man, born to be the Savior of men.

On the facade of the current church, near the top, stand fourteen statues, each about seven meters high, on either side of the central one representing Christ the Savior. The idea of the saving Word, who is the Son of God made man, is emphasized by the identity of these figures: John the Baptist, who in person and word is the

link between the Old Testament and the New; the Apostle John, whose Gospel witnesses to the life and word of the Lord, and the great doctors and theologians of the Church, who explained and studied that word more profoundly.

The church of San Giovanni in Laterano, as it appears to the visitor even from the decorations on its facade, is the symbol of the Church itself, which does not have words of its own to say but continues to propose the word of God, to which the pope and bishops are the faithful witnesses in historical time.

A Story of Disasters and Reconstruction

The history of the basilica of San Giovanni in Laterano is filled with mishaps large and small, some of them very grave. The real or presumed treasures that it was said the emperor Constantine had donated to it soon became legendary. Fantasy and fable grew to the point that it was said, and still is today, that the church was made all of gold. Thus it is natural that in 455, during the papacy of Leo I (440-461), Vandals headed by Genseric during their great sack of Rome directed their devastating fury toward this church. Whether

Raphael and workshop, *The Meeting of Pope Leo the Great with Attila*, detail. Vatican, Raphael Stanze (Stanza di Eliodoro)

On facing page, Pinturicchio, *Pius II enters the Lateran after his Coronation.* Siena, Libreria Piccolomini

real or presumed, very little of its treasure survived. The pope who in 452 was able to stop Attila could do nothing against these new barbarians except promise to restore the church immediately. In 896 an earthquake struck the cathedral of Rome, and Pope Sergius III (904-911) carried out extensive and necessary interventions for its consolidation.

Between 1308 and 1361, two fires seriously damaged the basilica. Pope Clement V (1304-1314), from his new papal residence in France, nonetheless continued to follow the situation of Rome Cathedral, and he had the first repairs made to the church. After the second fire, two popes, Urban V (1362-1370) and Gregory XI (1370-1378), saw to the reconstruction. What vandalism, earthquake, and fire could not do, was done by the neglect of men.

After Sixtus V, repairs and renovations of the church were insignificant, and San Giovanni remained in an evident state of disrepair until the middle of the XVIIth century, when Innocent X (1644-1655) ascended to the papal throne.

The XVIth and XVIIth centuries saw the most manifest works of restoration, and often of radical reconstruction, of the great monuments of the faith in Rome. Obviously, the artistic sensibilities expressed in the original works often yielded to the new taste of the time. The ancient Early Christian basilicas, Saint Peter's first of all, were remodeled or "embellished anew." The Baroque, solemn in style and redundant in form, is the final element in a journey that brought the churches a long distance from their early structures.

Pope Innocent X was the promoter of reconstruction of the new San Giovanni in Laterano. The occasion was the celebration of the Jubilee of 1650, and the architect was Francesco Borromini (1599-1667), one of the best-known artistic geniuses of the style known as Roman Baroque.

The enterprise appeared immediately to be a great challenge. The church was in the worst condition it had ever known and celebration of Holy Year was only six years away.

Borromini had to face numerous problems, and as always he managed to solve them brilliantly, usually in a fanciful, but always ingenious, way.

Diego Velázquez, *Portrait of Innocent X.* Rome, Galleria Doria Pamphilj

His task was extremely difficult because Innocent X insisted on preserving the Early Christian basilica as much as possible. But his desire could not be completely fulfilled because of the building's disastrous condition. Almost all the ancient columns of the nave had in preceding centuries been faced with bricks in order to reinforce the structure weakened by fires and earthquakes. Borromini presented three restoration plans to the pope, each of which offered various solutions for the necessary total renovation of the middle nave aisle. The one chosen was undoubtedly the most elegant. Twelve niches were created in the nave walls where, a few years later, statues of the Apostles were placed. The coat-of-arms of the Pamphilj family was set above the central arch. In the upper register on either side, large rectangular windows above the arches alternate with paintings in oval frames above every niche. The wooden ceiling installed in the XVIth century by Pius VI (1559-1565) was preserved, despite the architect's intention to construct a barrel vault and perhaps even a great dome. The side aisles were in such bad condition that they were torn down and rebuilt completely. Even though the interior decoration was done in a very short time, today it can be considered among Borromini's finest works. The enormous project was concluded in 1649 and the "new basilica" solemnly inaugurated on the occasion of the Holy Year of 1650, as intended. Before San Giovanni assumed completely the aspect it has today, more years had to pass, during which Borromini finished the interior and built the new facade.

The Architect of the New San Giovanni: Francesco Borromini

Francesco Borromini, *Self-Portrait.* Roma, church of San Carlo alle Quattro Fontane

Born in the Ticino area of Switzerland, Francesco Castelli, called Borromini (1599-1667), was for the first thirty years of his life a simple stonecutter and carver. A distant relative of Carlo Maderno (1556-1629), who designed the facade of Saint Peter's, he worked with Maderno on Saint Peter's and Palazzo Barberini. Notice of him and his work and his fortune as a prestigious architect came only after the death of his master. In 1634 he obtained his first public commission for the cloister, convent and church of San Carlo alle Quattro Fontane. His activity is distinguished by various projects; it reached the height of its prestige with the commissions for the restoration and transformation of San Giovanni in Laterano (1646) and construction of the church of Sant'Ivo alla Sapienza. Borromini worked mainly in Rome. He was a man of great learning and culture; at his death, some thousand books were found in his house, all hand-annotated by the artist. A great admirer of Michelangelo, whom he took as a role model and whose architecture he studied with great passion, Borromini was a complex personality. Irascible and intransigent in his dealings with patrons, in open dissent with Gian Lorenzo Bernini, whose cultural choices he did not share, he imbued his work, often not completely understood by his contemporaries, with his tormented spirituality. Today the solutions he adopted appear as truly new and prophetic, and technically astounding. In 1667 Borromini died by his own hand, putting an end to an existence that had given him more troubles than satisfaction.

Facade of San Giovanni in Laterano

The Current Facade

Just two years after his election, Pope Clement XII (1730-1740) opened competition for a design for the new facade of the basilica.

The project was too stimulating not to persuade the best artists and architects of the time to participate. The winning entry was presented by the Florentine Alessandro Galilei (1691-1736), leading architect of the Grand Duchy of Tuscany.

A scholar and theoretician of ancient architec-ture and of the XVIth century tradition from Michelangelo to Maderno, Galilei drew up a plan that reflected a rigorous, pragmatically anti-Baroque classicism. The result, for all to see, is a work undoubtedly monumental but not very graceful. Carlo Argan (1909-1993), the noted scholar and art critic, wrote: "Galilei repeats out of scale and in a monotonously uniform plane the scheme of late XVIth century Roman facades."

This work, carried out within three years (1732-1735), was realized practically at the same time as the plans for the Corsini Chapel also in San Giovanni in Laterano, built by

Clement XII, a member of the Corsini family. The facade is preceded by a brief flight of steps and looks onto the square with a five-arched two-story porch corresponding to the nave and four aisles of the church.

On one side of the porch, to the left as one enters, is the monumental *Statue of the Emperor Constantine*, founder of the basilica. The statue has been moved numerous times in the course of the centuries. Some scholars tend to believe that the subject is not Constantine but one of his sons; in any case, it was the intention of Clement XII, when he had the statue moved here in 1737, to honor the emperor whom tradition considers to be the first Christian emperor in history.

The second story of the porch is an arched loggia, and a rail running its full length crowns the facade. On the edge of the rail stand statues of saints, flanking the central figure of Christ whose hand is raised in blessing.

Piazza San
Giovanni in
Laterano, onto
which face the
Baptistry with its
unmistakable
octagonal shape,
the Papal

Benediction
Loggia, and on
the left, the
majestic bulk of
the Lateran
Palace designed
by Domenico
Fontana.

The Interior
of the Basilica

The visitor entering San Giovanni in Laterano sees a basilica with a nave flanked by two aisles on each side and a wide transept, and a large apse that was completely redone under Leo XIII (1878-1903). The decoration and architecture of the interior are the work of Borromini, and today the church is essentially as he conceived and decorated it. Once Borromini finished, little more was done to the church; some of the architectural elements date to the preceding basilica. The elaborate wooden ceiling immediately strikes the eye; it is the original one from the XVIth century, probably designed by Pirro Ligorio (1510-1583), the imaginative designer of the Villa d'Este garden at Tivoli. The ceiling, realized between 1562 and 1567, was restored under Pius VI (1775-1800), whose coat-of-arms is visible near the main entrance. The beautiful Cosmati-work floor dates to the papacy of Martin V (1417-1431) and was restored by Borromini. The striking features of the nave, which measures 130 meters from the door to the throne in the back of the apse, are the niches with statues of the Apostles, the very beautiful Gothic *baldacchino* above the altar, and the apse with mosaics completely redone in 1884.

However, before satisfying the visitor's legitimate curiosity as to details, we would like to draw his attention to the sense of the whole, for which Francesco Borromini's contribution was crucial. The artists coming after him, many of them highly intelligent, have found it an easy task to continue a project whose outlines had already been abundantly traced. Every element can seem unimportant and almost escape notice, yet the innovation of Borromini's work is this capacity to harmonize the parts into a whole that today, despite the heavy criticism of some historians, appears to us as the work of a great artistic genius.

The Nave

A simple description of the nave of the basilica can be helpful for grasping its various elements. The arches along the right and left sides lead into the side aisles, two on each side, containing funerary monuments, chapels, and altars.

On facing page, an evocative view of the basilica's interior and, right, a glimpse of the niches with statues of the apostles in the nave

Camillo Rusconi,
Saint John the
***Evangelist*, left,**
and *Saint Andrew*

Niches set into the pillars of the main nave hold imposing statues of the Apostles, made in the early years of the XVIIIth century by famous sculptors of the time such as Camillo Rusconi (1658-1728), responsible for four of the twelve statues, Pierre Legros (1666-1719), and Pierre Monnot (1657-1733).

Above the niches Alessandro Algardi (1595-1654) and some of his pupils depicted scenes from the Old and New Testaments. Higher still, between the windows, inside oval stucco garland-shaped frames, are paintings of prophets from the end of the XVIIth and beginning of the XVIIIth century. Two of them should be mentioned: Marco Benefial (1684-1764), the youngest and least known of the painters called to portray the prophets, and Sebastiano Conca (1680-1764). These artists tried, within the constraints of their epoch, to find a freer means of expression than was consonant with the pre-

vailing taste of the period. Even though the three levels of decoration of the nave were carried out in different moments, the idea sustaining them undoubtedly has a very strong unifying symbolic charge that, among other things, finds confirmation in a Church tradition present from its beginnings.

In the mosaics or frescoes of Early Christian churches, prophets and Apostles are represented in close relationship with each other, as these figures represent the continuity of the story of Salvation. They are, figuratively speaking, the voice of God that is present in human history in the Old and New Testaments. The meaningful Bible scenes placed in the center, more than acting as a link between the individual prophets and Apostles, signify that those "words" pronounced in the name of God have been given concrete form in the "events" of the history of Salvation.

In the Revelation and human history God not only speaks or has others speak, but he also acts. In an important document of Vatican Council II dedicted to the history of Salvation, we read: "The plan of Revelation is enacted with intimately connected events and words, in a way that the works accomplished by God in the history of Salvation manifest and reinforce the doctrine and meaningful reality of the words, and the words declare the works and clarify the mystery contained within them" (*Dei Verbum*, 2).

The nave of San Giovanni in Laterano makes visible what the Church has always considered to be the method God uses to intervene in human history.

The Transept and *Baldacchino*

The altar stands in the crossing between nave and transept, which was completely redone during the papacy of Clement VIII (1592-1605), following a design by Giacomo della Porta (1533-1602). We learn from documents that the newly elected pope wanted to restore the entire church but, discouraged by the slow pace of the Cavalier D'Arpino (1568-1640), to whom he had entrusted the direction of the painted decoration, he decided to remodel only the sacristy and the transept.

One of the most interesting aspects of the transept is the frescoes painted by some of the most famous Mannerist artists of the late XVIth century, including Orazio Gentileschi (1563-1639), Cesare Nebbia (c. 1536-1614), and Po-

View of the Chapel of the Choir

marancio (c. 1530-1592). The frescoes illustrate in a way simple and easy to understand the history of the basilica, indissolubly linked with the legendary events of Constantine's life and his "evident" conversion to Christianity. The decoration is arranged on two registers. At the top are represented the Apostles and the Fathers of the Church; below are panels with the story of the foundation of the basilica. The images are set in illusional tapestries with rich, ornate borders.

As coordinator, the Cavalier D'Arpino reserved for himself the painting of the large fresco of *The Ascension*, placed above the altar of the Blessed Sacrament. In this *Ascension* can be read the conclusion of the iconographical program of the transept. Jesus rising into heaven leaves as his visible representative the Church, whose primacy and authority are recognized also by the potentates of the earth, symbolized by Constantine.

The Gothic canopy built under Urban V, decorated with fresco panels attributed to Barna da Siena

The Cavalier D'Arpino is buried in the basilica, in the long hallway leading to the sacristy.

Another highlight of the transept which inevitably attracts the visitor's eye is the beautiful *baldacchino* made during the reign of Urban V (1362-1370), a pope of French origin who is venerated as Blessed by the Church; for the construction of this work, he received financial assistance from King Charles V of France (1338-1380).

Under the *baldacchino*, at the foot of the papal altar, a double staircase leads to the *Confessio*, the place where the relics are preserved of what, according to tradition, is the ancient wooden altar on which popes celebrated from the first to the fourth centuries, thus it is also the altar used by Saint Peter.

Independently of its historical and scientific truth, which is hard to prove, this altar can give a sense of the intimate relationship uniting San Giovanni in Laterano, the first seat of the papacy, and Saint Peter's basilica, which holds the cathedra of the first pope. As confirmation of the ideal and intimate relationship between the two basilicas, and widening to take in the other two major basilicas of Rome, San Paolo fuori le Mura and Santa Maria Maggiore, are other cogent connections, present in the middle section of the *baldacchino*. Beyond the metal grill are relics of the heads of Saint Peter and Saint Paul, and just below, on the four sides, are painted scenes from the life of the Virgin. Thus the *baldacchino* of San Giovanni in Laterano sums up the Church's entire reality which the other three basilicas narrate according to their own specific sense: the Church recognizes itself in the Eucharist, the celebration of the death and resurrection of Jesus the Savior, and like the Apostles it announces the word of newness and Salvation that the Son of God, made man and born of the Virgin Mary, has brought to all men of good will.

An inscription at the base of the paintings recalls that Pius IX (1846-1878) is the pope who "had [the *baldacchino*] restored and returned to its ancient splendor," in 1851. The author of the original work is Giovanni di Stefano (end of the XIVth century); Barna da Siena painted the twelve panels between 1367 and 1368, and they were restored and retouched a century later by Antoniazzo Romano (known from 1461 to 1508). The two reliquaries date from the XIXth century and substitute the XIVth century originals. Recently a noteworthy wooden statue of the precursor of Christ, *Saint John the Baptist*, has been placed in the crypt; attributed until the last century to Donatello (1386-1466), it is now thought to be the work of the lesser known painter and sculptor Donato da Formello (XIVth century).

The Apse

In all ancient basilicas, especially Early Christian ones, the area of the chancel with the cathedra and altar was the site of art *par excellence*. The starting point for builders of that time, more than the aesthetic, was the theological concept. If the center and fulcrum of the church is the altar, this had to be given a privileged position with respect to the rest of the church, and if artistic decoration was involved, it had to function to communicate immediately this idea of centrality. In following epochs, especially after the liturgy had lost some of its reference to the essentiality and functionality of

Donatello (workshop), *Tomb of Martin V*

**Francesco Grandi,
*Innocent III
Recognizes the
Franciscan Rule***

the signs and symbols of the celebrations, all the space of the church offered a place for embellishment, and the magnificence of certain interiors ended up distracting the faithful from the natural referent of the celebration.

In the case of San Giovanni in Laterano all this is evident, perhaps even more than in the other major basilicas. Too many things, some of them worthy in their own right, distract from the whole, and especially from the chancel and apse which seem hidden and diminished. It is true that at least from an artistic point of view these are very interesting elements, but it should be clear that a church is never just a museum or a collection of art works, but the place where a community celebrates its faith.

The chancel and apse were completely redone in 1884, during the papacy of Leo XIII. Rather than recover the ancient apse dating to the time

of Nicholas IV (XIIIth century), the architect Virginio Vespignani (1808-1882), who had already restored the *baldacchino* of the papal altar, had it torn down, along with its original mosaic by Jacopo Torriti, of which only a part survives.

The mosaics we see today are only a crude copy of the earlier ones. Torriti, who is the probable author of some frescoes in the Upper Church of San Francesco in Assisi and also of the mosaics in the apse of Santa Maria Maggiore with the *Coronation* and *Stories from the Life of the Virgin*, reveals himself to be here too a continuer of the most authentic Early Christian and Byzantine tradition. His style is hardly visible in the new XIXth century mosaic, which, although faithfully reproducing the iconography of the ancient composition, does not succeed in imparting its stylistic richness.

Mosaic in the vault of the apse, nineteenth century restoration of the mosaic by Jacopo Torriti

The mosaic depicts the patron of the work, Pope Nicholas IV, a Franciscan as shown by the two smaller figures portrayed at the sides of Mary and John the Baptist: Francis of Assisi and Anthony of Padua, the two most important saints of the order. The pope is shown at the Virgin's feet, kneeling in prayer with his hands lifted as a sign of offering. In a similar pose are the other figures, represented much larger to indicate their "greater" sainthood: the Virgin Mary, Saints Peter and Paul on the right of the jeweled cross; Saints John the Baptist, John the Evangelist, and Andrew, Peter's brother, on the left.

At the center of the apse ceiling is the face of the Savior, surrounded by angels, and below, the jeweled cross, symbol of his death and resurrection, bathed by the water pouring from the beak of the Dove, symbol of the Holy Spirit.

The water streams out from the cross in four springs; deer and sheep drink from it, and it renews all of creation represented by plants and flowers, animals and men shown in the activities of their daily life, symbolized by the ideal city of Jerusalem depicted at the foot of the Cross.

A symbolic reading of the mosaic is not hard to understand: Baptism brings about for the world and man a new creation. Just as water is the source of life, so does Baptism introduce Christians into the new life that Christ has claimed by his death and resurrection.

The Tombs of the Popes and Cardinals

When Borromini began the arduous task of re-building the interior of the basilica, many of the works that were already in it, mainly tombs of popes and cardinals, were dismantled and moved into the cloister. Pope Innocent X, in fact, wanted them to be moved back into the church as soon as the work was finished. The architect, for very good reasons, did not agree; he was afraid that the old medieval tombs would not be suited to the style of the "new" basilica. The idea that Borromini intended to carry out, if he had been able to operate in total liberty, was too revolutionary to be able to accept even just the hypothesis of a hybrid or compromise solution. We know, for example, that he meant to replace the XVIth century wooden ceiling of the nave with a barrel vault, but also that he wanted to destroy the Gothic ciborium and substitute a new one designed by him. The situation, however, required a balance that harmonized the two opposing demands of conservation and renewal. Borromini, as only he could have done, with the personality that all, at least today, recognize as his, found a solution to these two antithetical points of view.

Some important fragments of the antique monuments were conserved and inserted into a new tomb built *ex novo*. Work, however, proceeded slowly, interrupted and made difficult by the pope, who missed no chance to raise doubts and problems. Innnocent X's death in 1655 removed numerous obstacles. The new pope, Alexander VII (1655-1667), revealed himself to be more cooperative with Borromini, who was able to face his job with renewed serenity.

In the outside walls of the side aisles were oval windows, against which tombs could not be placed. Borromini incorporated the windows into the new tombs, making them seem like integral elements of the design. More than words, however, here we should give examples.

In the far right aisle, the *Funerary Monuments to Cardinal Martino de Chaves* (†1447) and *Cardinal Casati* († 1287) are worthy of special note. In the first, the only elements of the ancient tomb are the figure stretched out on the sarcophagus and other sculptures attributed to Isaia da Pisa (active between 1447 and 1464); the rest is Borromini's work. The second monument is even more unusual: only the marble plaque with the inscription belonged to Cardinal Giussano's old tomb. The Gothic tablets in the shape of two-light windows were originally on an altar in the chapel dedicated to Saint Mary Magdalene. Using these elements, Borromini created an original composition with illusional perspective, formed by a cusped architrave with ascending sides, so that the curves of all three sections play against the oval of the window. The architrave is supported by four "hooded herms," of which the middle two are smaller in order to accentuate the illusional effect of the perspective.

Funerary Monument to Cardinal Martin de Chaves

Fresco Attributed to Giotto

Another example of this process of blending old with new is the *Monument to Boniface VIII*, into which Borromini inserted an earlier fresco. The ancient Benediction Loggia which was destroyed contained this fragment, that was originally certainly much larger and made up perhaps of two more scenes: the baptism of the emperor Constantine and the construction of the early basilica of San Giovanni in Laterano.

It is not difficult to establish that the figure represented is Boniface VIII (1295-1303), the pope of the first Jubilee Year in Christian history; his name appears on the cartouche held up by the figure to the left of the pope.

As to the historical event commemorated in the monument and its author, instead, hypotheses differ. Some feel that the image can be connected with the solemn proclamation of the first Holy Year; others, much more recently, say that it documents the pope's taking possession of the Lateran complex in 1295. A confirmation of this latter hypothesis could come from the identity of the figure to the right of the pope; his physiognomy resembles that of Cardinal Matteo Rosso Orsini, who supported the election of Boniface VIII and was his closest collaborator in the life and policies of his papacy. In an illuminated manuscript (*Vaticano Latino* 4933), Cardinal Orsini, portrayed as he places the tiara on the head of the new pope, has in fact the same facial features as the person shown here.

Opinion is also divided concerning

Monument to Pope Boniface VIII with fragment of fresco by Giotto representing Boniface VIII Proclaiming the First Jubilee from the Lateran Loggia

attribution of the painting to Giotto (1267?-1337). Some see it as linked to the figure and workshop of Pietro Cavallini (doc. from 1273 to 1321) because of similarities with the frescoes on the inner facade of Santa Cecilia in Trastevere, while others lean more strongly toward Giotto, after restoration in 1956 made it possible to analyze the style. The fresco, nonetheless, above and beyond art historical hypotheses, is an important document for linking the Lateran basilica to the celebration of jubilee years. Boniface VIII, in fact, proclaimed the first Christian jubilee in history right here in San Giovanni in Laterano.

The Cloister

At the end of the left aisle of the church, one passes into the cloister, a beautiful square structure with flower beds in the center, constructed probably between 1215 and 1232 by the Vassalletto family, as declared in the inscription under the portico near the entrance, discovered during XIXth century restorations: "Vassalletto, instructed in the nobility of this art, began with his father the work that he finished alone." The portico is formed on all four sides by small arches supported by paired columns varying in form, some decorated with mosaics, and all with different capitals. Worthy of special note is the entablature decorated with an elegant mosaic frieze, and the eaves ornately carved with ani-

The XIIIth century cloister, by Vassalletto, with detail of the frieze

mals' heads. At the center of the courtyard, from which the imposing brick facade of the left arm of the transept can be admired, is a IXth century well. The vaults of the ambulatories rest on Ionic columns from a later period.

The four porticoes contained numerous fragments from the early basilica, such as the remains of Nicholas IV's cathedra, which was once in the apse, and a female head in stone from the Vth century, believed by some to be a portrait of Saint Helen, mother of the emperor Constantine. These were placed here by Borromini, as mentioned above, during the reign of Innocent X, with the idea of reutilizing them, at least in part, after restoration of the church was concluded.

Notable is the remnant of the *Tomb of Cardinal Annibaldi* (XIIIth century), attributed to Arnolfo di Cambio (c. 1245-1302), the Tuscan sculptor who left works in all four of the major basilicas of Rome, among them the well-known bronze statue of the Apostle Peter in the Vatican, the monumental ciborium in San Paolo fuori le Mura, and the crèche in Santa Maria Maggiore.

The Baptistry

I n ancient Early Christian basilicas, only the cathedral had a baptistry. Baptism, in fact, was administered directly in the cathedrals, by the bishops in the dioceses and by the pope in Rome. Only much later (VII-VIIIth centuries), with the growth of churches in the countryside and parishes in the cities, did these churches also obtain baptismal fonts.

The cathedral of the diocese of Rome was San Giovanni in Laterano, so that its baptistry was the first and oldest in Rome and in all the West.

To reach it, one must go out of the basilica through a door at the end of the right transept, cross part of the portico designed and built by Domenico Fontana (1543-1607) for Sixtus V, and then walk past a XIXth century building on the left constructed under Leo XIII. Tradition claims that the baptistry, dedicated to Saint John the Baptist, was founded by Constantine in the IVth century, probably transforming the structure of a nymphaeum in a Roman house.

Sixtus III (432-440) had it completely remodeled and added an atrium. Hilarius (461-468) built three chapels: two, almost completely transformed, still exist, while the third was demolished by Domenico Fontana during renovations of the square. Paul III (1534-1549) had the dome demolished and the current ciborium built, covered by a pitched roof. The last restoration was carried out by Borromini during the papacy of Alexander VII. The interior is on an octagonal plan; at the center eight prophyry columns set in a circle, with Ionic, Corinthian, and composite capitals, support an architrave on which rests a second register of

The Baptistry, known as San Giovanni in Fonte

Francesco Penni, *The Baptism of Constantine,* **detail. Vatican, Raphael Stanze (Sala di Costantino). The scene is set in the Lateran baptistry**

In the chapels and oratories annexed to the main area of the church are fragments and works in mosaic from the VIth and VIIth centuries.

Of special interest is the mosaic vault of the Chapel of Saint John the Evangelist, founded by Pope Hilarius. In the center stands the Lamb, symbol of the Risen Christ. In other mosaics from the same period, for example in basilicas in Ravenna, in the place of the Lamb is the jeweled cross, symbol of Christ's death and resurrection. The two symbols, different in form but identical in content, underline, also by their location, the centrality of Jesus Christ in the history of Salvation.

The other mosaic is the one in the Oratorio di San Venanzio, begun by Pope John IV (640-642) and completed under Pope Theodore I (642-649). Built to honor the memory and preserve the relics of the Dalmatian saints Venantius and Domnio, its apse is still today decorated with original mosaics. At the center is the Blessing Christ between two angels, with below the Virgin Mary and at her sides

Two views of the interior of the Baptistry with the basalt basin and its rich bronze covering

smaller marble columns. At the center of the baptistry is a green basalt basin covered by a XVIIth century bronze gable.

The paintings in the drum are copies made in 1960 of the original XVIIth century canvases by Andrea Sacchi; they portray scenes from the life of Saint John the Baptist, the Precursor of Christ. The wall frescoes with stories of Constantine were painted in the XVIIth century by Andrea Camassei (1602-1649) and Carlo Maratta (1625-1713).

the Apostles Peter and Paul, John the Baptist, John the Evangelist, the two martyrs to whom the oratory is dedicated, and the two popes who had it built. Other saints in the apse arch, four on either side, complete the series. Above, in two panels are represented in mosaic the symbols of the four Evangelists, and on the outer sides of the front wall the cities of Jerusalem and Bethlehem.

Noteworthy in this chapel is also the beautiful XVIth century wooden ceiling.

Mid-VIIth century mosaic, *The Blessing Christ between Two Angels*. Oratory of San Venanzio

Mid-VIIth century
mosaic, *Saints
Maurus and
Septimianus.*
Oratory of
San Venanzio

Toward the Obelisk and Beyond

Coming out of the baptistry of San Giovanni in Laterano, inevitably the eye falls on the great obelisk which, with its 32 meters of height and 522 tons of weight, is the most imposing of Rome's obelisks and of those made of granite from Egyptian quarries. Transported from Egypt during the reign of the emperor Constantine and erected by his son Constantine II on the longitudinal axis of the Circus Maximus around 357, it was consecrated as a symbol of the victory of Christianity over the ancient cults, as indicated by a four-line poem carved in its base and now lost, but which was copied and handed down to us by a learned man of the XVIth century, Michele Mercati.

Buried for several centuries, the obelisk was discovered in 1587 broken into three pieces. The three fragments were put back together and the obelisk raised between 6 July and 3 August 1588. Pope Sixtus V consecrated it on 10 August of that year, installing at its top a bronze cross. This same pope, as part of the radical urban renewal of Rome, arranged for the great consular roads to converge on the basilica of San Giovanni in Laterano. Thus the obelisk created an ideal historical line indissolubly uniting the ancient civilizations with Christianity through the symbols of their power. The obelisk, sign of the greatness of ancient Egypt, and the consular roads which had led the ancient Roman legions to the conquest of Europe found their point of convergence in the pope's cathedral and the baptistry that still today stands at its side. The ancient Pharaohs and the emperors rep-

The ancient Egyptian granite obelisk placed in Piazza San Giovanni in Laterano

resenting false gods, albeit unknowingly, end up adoring the true God, of whom the pope, according to the heightened political and theological sensibility of the time, was the representative on earth.

The cross on the obelisk and the conversion of the last great Roman emperor, who according to the inscription at the base of the monolith was baptized here, functioned to testify that ancient history is here fully accomplished, and that all human history in the sign of Christ who died and rose again realized in him its complete, all-encompassing fullfillment.

There is a detail which could escape the notice of those looking up from below, but which can be seen from the Benediction Loggia, the upper part of the small facade on the back of the basilica. From this position one can see that the facade, the work of Domenico Fontana in 1568, looks directly at the obelisk and thus is in almost perfect line with the basilica of Santa Maria Maggiore visible at the end of what is now Via Merulana. It does not take too much imagination to think that all this was part of a specific plan.

The pope's cathedral, dedicated originally to the Savior, is linked ideally with Santa Maria Maggiore to emphasize by the close relationship between the two churches the intimate bond between the Mother and her Son.

Our suggestion to the pilgrim who wants to visit these two basilicas is to cover this distance on foot, starting from Santa Maria Maggiore. Also on an emotional level it will seem to him to be covering the history of millennia, which from man's origins, his experiences and cultures, leads him to the encounter with the one who is the focal point of history: the Savior, celebrated in the cathedral of the pope.

Its History

The basilica of San Paolo fuori le Mura is, after Saint Peter's, the largest church in Rome. Its imposing monumentality is made even more evident by the great space separating it from the buildings around it.

Erected in the first half of the IVth century by the emperor Constantine on the spot indicated by tradition as the tomb of the Apostle Paul, it has always and unceasingly been the goal of the faithful and pilgrims coming from all over the world to venerate the "Apostle to the Gentiles."

The church remained practically intact in its evocative aspect of an Early Christian patriarchal basilica until the early XIXth century, when it was almost completely destroyed by a terrible fire (1823).

The appearance of the monument as it stands today, the precious materials embellishing it, the undeniable solemnity and austerity conferred on the complex after a long and arduous work of rebuilding, seem nonetheless not enough to cancel out the memory of what the ancient basilica must have looked like. Paintings and engravings remain to bear witness to that earlier building.

The origin of the "memory" of Paul is linked to the deposition of the Apostle in the area called "ad aquas Salvias," today known as "Tre Fontane," or "Three Fountains," not far from the left bank of the Tiber, on the Via Ostiense about two kilometers from the Aurelian walls. After his martyrdom (A.D. 67), Paul's body was laid in a "cella memoriae," a tomb, just as had been the case with the Apostle Peter. After the edict of 314 that freed the practice of Christianity, Constantine built a place of worship above the simple tombs of each of these Apostles. The one dedicated to Saint Paul was consecrated, according to tradition, on 18 November 324 by Pope Sylvester I.

The building was certainly not solemn and majestic like the one dedicated to the memory of Saint Peter, so that in the same century the emperors Valentinian II (371-392), Theodosius (347-395), and Arcadius (377-408) decided to exalt Saint Paul's tomb with greater magnificence, building a new basilica which was called "of the three emperors." Pope Siricius (384-399) consecrated it in 390.

The new church was an imposing structure divided into a nave and four aisles, marked off by 80 colossal marble columns. Galla Placidia (c. 390-450), the daughter of Theodosius and sister of the emperor Onorius (395-423), had it decorated with the great mosaic on the triumphal arch, still visible today despite its reworking between the VIIIth and IXth centuries and subsequently restored several times.

The basilica's location near the banks of the Tiber made it subject to numerous pirate raids, like that of the Longobards in 739 and the Saracens in 847, who sacked it of many art works and precious objects. For fear of other raids, Pope John VIII (872-882) had a fort built around the church; inside it a small hamlet soon grew up, which took the name of Johannipolis from the name of the pope. The same thing had happened a few years earlier for Saint Peter's in the Vatican, where Leo IV (847-855) built walls, still today called "Leonine," to protect the church.

The first works of restoration of the basilica began around the Vth century. From then on, a series of renovation and beautification campaigns was carried out by various popes, always connected with the cult of the Apostle Paul; in particular, Gregory the Great (590-604) and Leo III (795-816) worked to arrange the area around the altar and to embellish the interior with precious furnishings. During the XIth century San Paolo was enriched with two important works: a belltower which, saved from the fire in 1823, was later demolished to make room for a more

Detail of the mosaic of *Saint Paul* on the back wall of the triumphal arch

On facing page, Pietro Francesco Garola, *Interior of the Basilica of San Paolo*. Turin, Galleria Sabauda

Pages 92-93, the triumphal arch of Galla Placidia and the vault of the apse decorated with mosaics

modern one, and a bronze Byzantine portal of rare beauty set into the main entrance, donated in 1070 by Pantaleone of Amalfi. The portal was moved in 1967 and today closes the Holy Door.

The XIIIth century was the period of the basilica's greatest splendor, seeing the creation of the Easter candlestick by Nicola d'Angelo and Pietro Vassalletto, the mosaic decoration of the apse, and the beautiful cloister.

During the reign of Pope John XXII (1316-1334), Pietro Cavallini (known from 1273 to 1321) painted the frescoes in the nave, and Arnolfo di Cambio (c. 1245-1302) sculpted the ciborium on the high altar. But already by the beginning of the XIVth century the church was showing signs of the passage of time and neglect, and Pope Boniface IX (1389-1404) decreed that part of the sum gathered from the sale of indulgences would be earmarked for restoration of the basilica.

Over the centuries the popes' attention to the church was unceasing, with works of restoration or decoration.

In this sense, Clement VIII (1592-1605) particularly stands out. He had new altars built, among them one to Saint Bridget and the high altar attributed to Onorio Longhi. He also gave Carlo Maderno (1556-1629) the commission for the Chapel of the Blessed Sacrament, now dedicated to Saint Lawrence, one of the first Christian martyrs, put to a slow death, according to tradition, on a burning grate.

In 1724 the Chapel of the Crucifix was built, in which was placed the miraculous XIVth century Crucifix, attributed in the past to Pietro Cavallini and today considered a work of the Sienese school.

Reconstruction after the Fire

The most dramatic event, however, which meant that the basilica had practically to be rebuilt, happened in the night between the 15th and 16th of July 1823. A violent fire, perhaps caused by a lack of caution on the part of workers repainting the roof, destroyed almost completely the sacred building and its precious contents.

The many people who came running to the church were shocked at the spectacle of flames, smoke, and ash which, as an eyewitness wrote, "seemed like a terrrible Vesuvius." News of the disaster was kept from Pope Pius VII (1800-1823), who was on his deathbed (he died a month later, on 20 August), thus leaving to his successor, Leo XII (1823-1829), the heavy burden of rebuilding.

In the months to come, an ardent debate arose

The Apostle to the Gentiles: Paul

Paul is the Apostle most responsible for the spread of Christianity throughout the Greek and Roman world. His Epistles and the Biblical book of the Acts of the Apostles give us abundant information about his life, thought, and activities. No other Apostle is so well documented.

Born in Tarsus, a town in Cilicia whose inhabitants enjoyed the privilege of recognition as Roman citizens, into a Jewish family around the year 10 B.C., he was in the beginning a zealous and relentless persecutor of the burgeoning Christian movement.

Converted on the road to Damascus by a vision of the Risen Christ, he became the most fervent proclaimer of the Christian faith. His preaching took him to Cyprus, Pamphylia, Pisidia, and Lycaonia.

Fourteen years after his conversion, he participated actively in the first council of the Church in Jerusalem where, with his decisive contribution, the principle was established that Jewish law did not obligate pagan converts to Christianity to undergo Jewish rites (for example, circumcision). On that occasion, he received from the other disciples official recognition as the Apostle to the Gentiles.

Leaving Jerusalem again, he made two journeys covering practically all the great cities of the time on the Greek and Middle Eastern coasts of the Mediterranean.

In the year 58 he was arrested in Jerusalem and held prisoner in Caesarea until 60, when the Roman procurator Festus sent him to the imperial capital to be judged. In 63 he was found innocent and freed, whereupon he set out on new travels, perhaps arriving in Spain, which was the farthest reach of the known world at the time. In about 67, he was imprisoned again in Rome, for the last time, ending in his martyrdom. Tradition says that he was beheaded, and a legend tells that his head, when it was severed from his body, bounced three times on the ground giving rise to three fountains. On the presumed site of his martyrdom a church was built, called the "Tre Fontane," or "Three Fountains." His body was buried in the necropolis on the Via Ostiense. The saint's relics are today venerated in the crypt of the basilica dedicated to him.

Flemish XVIth century tapestry of *Saint Paul Preaching in Athens*. Vatican, Picture Gallery

concerning the process to be followed for its reconstruction, in which famous architects, archeologists, and scholars took part. Two opposing factions formed, between those who favored a faithful reconstruction of the original and those proposing a completely new building. Among these latter was the architect Giuseppe Valadier (1762-1839), whose plans led him to be named for a brief time head of the reconstruction project. However, on 23 November 1825, the special committee for the reconstruction decided to entrust the work to the architect Pasquale Belli (1752-1833), who with his co-workers had expressed an opinion in favor of reconstruction respecting the original structure of the basilica, in line with the wishes of the pope.

In 1833, at Belli's death, Luigi Poletti (1792-1869) took the direction of the work in hand and brought it essentially to its conclusion.

The project maintained the Early Christian architectural layout, but involved the destruction

The Pope of the Current Basilica of San Paolo: Leo XII

A month after the death of his predecessor Pius VII, Cardinal Annibale Sermattei della Genga, who had been vicar of Rome for three years, was elected pope, taking the name of Leo XII (1823-1829).

The new pope was immediately faced with the task of rebuilding San Paolo, which had been practically destroyed in the night between the 15th and 16th of July, two months before his election.

His strong, decisive character, the distinguishing personality trait of this pope who governed the Church with an authoritarian and conservative manner, was certainly helpful to him in taking over quickly and with determination the project of a reconstruction that was difficult both for the building in itself and for the political moment in which Europe found itself just then.

In the Holy Year of 1825 - which the pope, despite the negative opinion of numerous people, insisted on decreeing, and which in effect revealed itself to be a religious success beyond everyone's expectations - Leo XII invited all the world's bishops to make Christians aware of the opportunity to rebuild the basilica dedicated to the Apostle Paul.

Two tendencies opposed each other in the choice of criteria for its reconstruction. There were those, like the pope, who tended toward a plan respecting the shape of the Early Christian basilica, and others instead who proposed construction of a completely new building. It is easy to guess that, given the nature of his character, the pope's opinion was determinant in the decision. On 10 December 1854 Pope Pius IX (1846-1878) was able to consecrate the "new" San Paolo, but many more years were to pass before the church was truly finished.

of a large part of the medieval traces evident in the basilica. On 5 December 1854, Pope Pius IX (1846-1878) consecrated the altar of the Confession, and on 10 December of the same year the new basilica.

Many years still had to pass, however, before San Paolo could appear as it does today. Work continued both outside with the mosaics of the new facade, construction of the porticoed court and the baptistry, and inside with the painted decoration of the side walls of the nave, the new series of papal portraits in mosaic, and the fresco cycle of scenes from the life of Saint Paul. The concluding episode in the story of the long reconstruction of San Paolo fuori le Mura was the move of the Byzantine door in 1967 to its current position as the Holy Door. Thus: "Rising from the ashes of the terrible fire of 1823 and rebuilt on its ancient foundations, in over a century of work with contributions pouring in from all over the world, in full accordance with the message of the Apostle to the Gentiles, the new basilica of San Paolo, both on its exterior and interior, presents itself as the 19th century reinterpretation of a classical-Christian temple, in its proportions, choice of materials, in its color and light" (Krautheimer, 1980).

The new basilica, on a Latin cross plan, is divided into a nave and four aisles by 4 rows of 20 columns each. It is 131 meters long, 65 meters wide, and 30 meters high.

The Exterior

As in the Early Christian basilica, the church of San Paolo is entered through a square court. Today's atrium, however, with its 70 meters per side and 146 columns, is much larger and more imposing than its predecessor. Designed by Luigi Poletti around 1868, it was built between 1890 and 1928 by Guglielmo Calderini (1837-1916). In the center a statue of a severe Saint Paul, the work of Giuseppe Obici (1807-1878), rises among flower beds and palm trees. The Apostle holds in one hand a sword, the symbol of his martyrdom, and in the other a book to emphasize his activity as proclaimer of the Word of God, both in writing and orally. Saint Paul appears again on the fa-

cade of the church on the left hand of Christ enthroned; on the right is Saint Peter.

The mosaic, made by the Studio Vaticano between 1854 and 1874 following cartoons by Filippo Agricola (1795-1857) and Nicola Consoni (1814-1884), is a mannered work, typical of the XIXth century and distant from the spirit and liveliness of Early Christian mosaics. In the center, Christ is represented as the Lamb of God, standing on a mount; from it spring forth

Two views of the basilica of San Paolo with the portico in the foreground

four streams where twelve lambs drink symbolizing the Church founded on the twelve Apostles. In the background are the holy cities of Jerusalem and Bethlehem. The prophets Isaiah, Jeremiah, Ezekiel, and Daniel, the major Old Testament heralds of the Savior, appear between the windows below. At the bottom of the facade is the wide vestibule, distinguished by its coffered ceiling, that through three portals gives access to the interior of the basilica.

The Doors

In the liturgy of the Church, the door has not only a functional but also a symbolic value. In the Gospels, Christ himself says he is the door leading to "fertile pastures," a clear reference to a life that continues after death.

For this reason, often church doors were and are adorned with reliefs, some the work of great artists, beautiful not only in an aesthetic

On facing page, the facade of San Paolo with its mosaic realized by the Studio Vaticano

Teodoro di Costantinopoli, Byzantine door, detail

The Architect of the New San Paolo: Luigi Poletti

Luigi Poletti (1792-1869) was born in Modena. He received his early training in the art and techniques of architecture at the Accademia Clementina in Bologna.

In 1818, with the financial assistance of the duke of Modena, he was able to continue and conclude his studies in Rome, collaborating also with Raffaele Stern (1764-1820), who in those years was building the new wing of the Museo Chiaramonti in the Vatican.

This activity brought him to the attention of the Holy See, who awarded him various commissions.

In 1833, while he was working on the restoration of the Lateran Palace, he was offered the possibility of taking over supervision of the work on the basilica of San Paolo, which had been practically destroyed by a fire. This job can be considered the most complex and important of Poletti's life, and it kept him busy until his death.

In his reconstruction of the basilica, Poletti took abundant inspiration from his studies of Roman classicism.

The monument which is today visible to all, while grandiose in form, seems quite cold and distant from the spirit of the Early Christian basilica. Poletti, who was also responsible for rebuilding Santa Maria degli Angeli in Assisi, destroyed by an earthquake in 1832, and the famous monument in Piazza Navona in Rome dedicated to the Immaculate Conception (1854-1856), can be remembered as one of the principal masters of architecture working in Rome and in Italy in the middle of the XIXth century.

Antonio Maraini, middle door of the basilica

sense but also functional in terms of Christian symbolism.

Of the three doors from the narthex into the basilica, the oldest, as well as the most important, is the one on the right looking at the facade. It is called simply the Byzantine door because of its unmistakable style. As said above, it was originally the central portal of the basilica, then after the restoration of the church occasioned by the extensive damage suffered in the 1823 fire, it was placed in its current position, closing the Holy Door, in 1967.

The author of what is considered one of the most beautiful doors of its kind in existence is one Theodore of Constantinople. Inscriptions report also the name of the bronze foundryman, Staurachio, the date 1070, and the patron, the Amalfi consul Pantaleone, portrayed in one of the 54 panels making up the door.

The House of Pantaleone was one of the most illustrious in Amalfi. It is known that the consul commissioned, also in Constantinople, two other important bronze doors: one for Amalfi Cathedral and one for the sanctuary of Saint Michael Archangel at Monte Sant'Angelo. It is also known that his father had a celebrated door made for the abbey of Montecassino.

The panels of damascened silver narrate, from the top, the birth of Christ from the Nativity to the Pentecost, followed by images of the prophets and Apostles. Evident references are made to the Byzantine iconography of well-known mosaic cycles, particularly in the scene of the Crucifixion.

Particularly beautiful and refined are the two eagles in the two panels at the bottom corners of the door.

The main door to the basilica, also of bronze, is gigantic, measuring 7.48 meters high and 3.35 meters wide; it was wrought between 1929 and 1931 by the sculptor Antonio Maraini (1886-1963).

The Benedictine abbot Ildefonso Schuster, a noted liturgist and later archbishop of Milan, dictated the iconographical program. The striking feature of the door is a large cross adorned with vine tendrils and damascened images of the Apostles and the symbols of the four Evangelists. At the sides of the cross, in five plaques per side, are narrated episodes from the presence of Peter and Paul in Rome, concluding with the martyrdom of the two saints. Of special note are the two images of Christ, in embossed silver to give him special emphasis, in the center of the two panels of the door. In the one on the right, Jesus names Peter head of the Church, and on the left He converts Paul on the road to Damascus.

Teodoro di Costantinopoli, Byzantine door, detail of the panel with an eagle

The Interior

The sense of monumental space emanating from the interior of one of the largest basilicas in the world is produced both by the symmetrical arrangment of the 80 white marble columns and by the mirror effect created by the floor.

The care and rigorous choice of details shown by Luigi Poletti in the interior decoration of the basilica of San Paolo does not succeed however, in the opinion of many people, in moving beyond a cold academic feeling.

The nave, flanked by two aisles on each side, rests on a floor that is elevated about 90 centimeters above the earlier one. Laid first in the transept, where also the precious marble slabs from the ancient basilica were re-utilized, and then in the nave, which alternates green marble squares and red granite circles, the floor contributes to giving a diffused sense of luminousness to the whole church.

The oldest part of the building, albeit subject to renovations and restoration, is the apse and triumphal arch, at the foot of which are placed statues of *Saints Peter* and *Paul* on marble bases. The monuments to the other Apostles are inserted into niches in the outer aisles. None of these statues is worthy of special attention, all of them being little more than academic exercises.

In the central section of the richly decorated ceiling stand out the coats-of-arms of the popes who contributed to rebuilding the new basilica.

Underneath, between the windows flanked by pilaster strips with Corinthian capitals, alternate wall paintings with *Stories from the Life of Saint Paul*. The 36 frescoes, illustrating stories from the *Acts of the Apostles*, were commissioned by Pius IX in 1857 to replace other paintings, of a much higher quality, by Pietro Cavallini, which were destroyed in the fire or removed by Pasquale Belli in 1828. The work

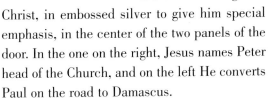

The nave looking
toward the
baldacchino

Pages 106-107,
view of the
transept with the
baldacchino in
the foreground

was concluded in only three years by a group of twenty-two artists, among whom the best known was Francesco Podesti (1800-1895).

Above each frame two winged cherubs hold the Latin inscription connected with the scene beneath it.

On the inner facade wall are six beautiful alabaster columns about 8 meters high. They were a gift for the reconstruction of the basilica from the Viceroy of Egypt, who offered them in 1840 to Gregory XVI. The two central columns support an architrave which in turn holds an imposing marble coat-of-arms of Pius IX, the work of Giosuè Meli.

One of the two malachite altars donated by Czar Nicholas I and placed at the ends of the transept

The Papal Portraits

Beneath the windows of the central and side aisles of the nave are the mosaic portraits of the popes from Saint Peter to today. It is a tradition that at the death of a pope the image of the newly elected pope is added to the series.

Pope Leo the Great (440-461) initiated the series, with the portraits painted in fresco. Only 41 of these early portraits survive, now detached and in the museum of the church.

In 1847 Pope Pius IX had the series recreated from the beginning, this time in mosaic; for the execution of the mosaics it was necessary to paint models, or *bozzetti*, in oil. Today these paintings are in the storerooms of the Fabbrica di San Pietro, which acquired the whole series once they were prepared. The work was supervised by Filippo Agricola, director of the Studio Vaticano del Mosaico. Beyond their indisputable iconographical value, these portraits respond also to historical and theological demands: first of all, that of dating the various pontificates, and then the need to make evident the apostolic succession from Peter to the current pope who is here revealed as the legitimate successor to the first Apostle and thus the most authoritative representative of Christ in the Church.

Cross-section of
the nave aisles
with tondo
portraits of
the popes

The mosaic on
the triumphal
arch and, in the
background, the
mosaic in the
apse

The Mosaics in the Apse

The mosaic decoration of the apse was seriously damaged in the 1823 fire. Restoration began only in 1836. Some original fragments which escaped damage were incorporated into the faithfully reproduced replica that was made to give new life to the ancient image; others, representing heads of the Apostles and birds, are still visible in the museum attached to the basilica.

The original mosaic was executed between the second and third decade of the XIIIth century by Venetian craftsmen called to Rome by Pope Honorius III.

Today, as then, at the center of the apse vault Christ sits on a throne set in a meadow rich in flowers and animals between Saints Peter and Andrew on the left, and on the right Paul and his early biographer, the Evangelist Luke, author of the Acts of the Apostles.

Prostrate at Christ's feet can be recognized a pope, dressed in a white chasuble and in a gesture of adoration and dedication; this is Honorius III, who commissioned the ancient mosaic.

In the lower register is the *Etimacia*, the empty throne with the instruments of the Passion: the cross, crown of thorns, and nails. Below this are five Holy Innocents and, kneeling, historical figures from the time of Honorius III: the sacristan Adinolfo and the abbot Giovanni Caetani. The importance of the mosaic in San Paolo lies in the fact that it marked the beginning of a revival, albeit short-lived, of the use of mosaics on a monumental scale, for centuries used in the decoration of churches and always at the service of the Faith and its content. In the apse of San Paolo, for example, it functioned to confirm the centrality of Jesus Christ in the plan of Salvation and to underline the life witness of the Apostles and saints who for him had put their own lives on the line.

It might seem unusual to see Paul on Christ's right hand, and thus in a privileged position with respect to Peter, but this is easily explained by the dedication of the basilica to the Apostle Paul.

The Mosaic on the Triumphal Arch of Galla Placidia

The mosaic of Galla Placidia (c. 390-450), so called from the name of the sister of the emperor Honorius, was created during the papacy of Leo the Great at the same time as the one in the basilica of Santa Maria Maggiore. Completely reconstructed in the VIIIth century, it was subsequently restored several times. The 1823 fire was a crucial factor in causing it to lose much of its ancient splendor.

The great mosaic on the arch describes almost literally the passage in the Revelation to Saint John, which narrates the first of his great prophetic visions: "After this I had a vision of an open door to heaven... In front of the throne was something that resembled a sea of glass like crystal. In the center and around the throne there were four living creatures... The first creature resembled a lion, the second was like a calf, the third had a face like that of a human being, and the fourth looked like an eagle in flight... Day and night they do not stop exclaiming: 'Holy, holy, holy is the Lord God Almighty, who was, and who is, and who is to come!'

Whenever the living creatures give glory and honor and thanks to the one who sits on the throne, who lives forever and ever, the twenty-four elders fall down before the one who sits on the throne and worship him, who lives forever and ever. They throw down their crowns before the throne, exclaiming: 'Worthy are you, Lord our God, to receive glory and honor and power, for you created all things; because of your will they came to be and were created" (*Revelation* 4:1, 6-11).

Once again Christ is described as the Savior and, assimilated to God the Father, becomes the judge of men and of history.

On the back wall of the triumphal arch was placed part of the mosaic decoration that

Back of the triumphal arch with restored original mosaics by Pietro Cavallini

Arnolfo di Cambio's baldacchino and detail of the two statues of *Saint Paul* and *Saint Peter* set in the corner niches adorned the ancient facade of the basilica, attributed to Cavallini in the XIVth century. In the center a clypeus held by two angels contains the image of the Blessing Christ.

On the ancient facade, between the windows, were portrayed also Saint Paul, the Virgin and Child, Saint John the Baptist, and Saint Peter.

The Ciborium

The ciborium, miraculously spared in the fire of 1823, a work of very high artistic quality, is the most important surviving witness to the medieval furnishings of the basilica.

Despite restorations which have become necessary from time to time, such as substitution of the four columns supporting it, the ciborium is essentially as Arnolfo di Cambio (1245-c. 1302) made it.

Built in 1285 on a commission from the abbot Bartolomeo (1282-1297), it is the effective testimony of a new sculptural language and of the introduction into late XIIIth century Rome of the new Gothic style. A structure rich in bas-reliefs and mosaic decorations rests on four columns of red porphyry. The bas-reliefs represent *Adam and Eve, Cain*

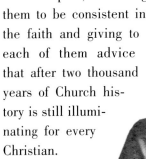

and Abel's Offerings, and *The Abbot Bartolomeo offering the Ciborium to Saint Paul*. In the niches on the sides are statues of Peter and Paul, Paul's disciple Timothy, and Saint Benedict, founder of the order which bears his name; in ancient times as now, Benedictine monks preside over the celebrations in the basilica and live in the adjoining monastery. Mosaic decoration in clypei reproduces animal figures.

The ciborium is placed over the papal altar. Below the altar is the Confession, the most sacred spot in the whole church, the tomb of the Apostle Paul. It is reached by a double staircase, surrounded by a white marble rail whose banisters reproduce the style typical of those in Early Christian basilicas.

Near Paul's tomb are also the mortal remains of Saint Timothy, who along with Titus was one of the Apostle's two favorite disciples. In three letters, two to Timothy and one to Titus, which the Church preserves among the revealed texts of the Holy Scriptures, Paul shows great love for his disciples, encouraging them to be consistent in the faith and giving to each of them advice that after two thousand years of Church history is still illuminating for every Christian.

The Easter Candlestick

A work of great art historical interest, which survived the fire, is the impressive marble candlestick near the papal altar on the left in the transept.

This type of marble candestick, created to hold the Easter candle, the symbol of Christ the "light of the world," began to be widely used beginning in the Xth century as part of the Holy Saturday liturgy.

The candleholder is imposing in size, 5.6 meters tall, with splendid decorations along its shaft. Divided horizontally into six registers, the decorations alternate vegetable and animal motifs with scenes of the Passion and Resurrection of Christ.

Below the Christological cycle is an inscription with the names of the two authors: Nicola D'Angelo and Pietro Vassalletto, noted marble sculptors of the early XIIIth century.

The Chapels

Four chapels open off the transept, created in different epochs but united in their facades by the same architectural structure.

These are the chapels of Saint Stephen, the Crucifix, Saint Lawrence, and finally, Saint Benedict.

The Chapel of Saint Stephen was designed by the architect Luigi Poletti during reconstruction of the transept, for which materials and marble from the ancient building were partially reutilized.

The chapel is dedicated to the deacon Saint Stephen, first martyr of the Church of Jerusalem. On the altar stands a statue of the saint by Rinaldo Rinaldi (1793-1873).

Next is the Chapel of the Crucifix, built by Benedict XIV for the Jubilee of 1725 to house the XIVth century *Crucifix* attributed to Tino da Camaino and to exhibit it for the veneration of the faithful. Today the chapel is used for custody and adoration of the Blessed Sacrament.

In the niche to the left of the entrance is a statue of *Saint Bridget* attributed to Stefano Maderno (1576-1636). The saint is shown kneeling and turned toward the Crucified Christ who, according to tradition, turned his head toward her as she knelt at his feet in prayer.

In the chapel is also a wooden statue of *Saint Paul* - somewhat mutilated because of the habit of pilgrims of taking a fragment of it as a relic and souvenir - and a very fine XIIIth century mosaic icon of the *Madonna and Child*.

A plaque near the altar recalls the fact that in front of this icon, on 22 August 1541, Saint Ignatius of Loyola professed his vows, initiating the activity of the Society of Jesus.

The icon is in the typical Byzantine pose of the

Theotokos Hodigitria, that is, the Mother of God who indicates the way, with her Son on her left arm. The Virgin, wrapped in a dark blue mantle, stands out from the gold ground; the Child is wrapped in a red cloak decorated with motifs imitating pearls and precious stones.

Chapel of the Choir or of Saint Lawrence

Page 115: XIIIth century mosaic, *Virgin and Child*. Chapel of the Crucifix

The structure and composition of the icon make clear its devotional function.

The third chapel, originally dedicated to the Blessed Sacrament, is now dedicated to the martyr Lawrence, one of the first and best known saints of the Church of Rome who, according to tradition, was martyred by being burned on a grate.

It seems that the chapel was built according to a design by the architect Carlo Maderno and inaugurated for the Jubilee of 1625.

Before the fire, the vault was frescoed with Sibyls and Prophets, the work of the Florentine Anastasio Fontebuoni (1571-1626), while it is known that the altarpiece was executed by Giovanni Lanfranco in 1621.

The painted decorations of the chapel were created by Antonio Vilegiardi (1869-1936) and document various episodes from the life of Saint Lawrence, while the lunette above the altar was painted in the middle of the XIXth century by Francesco Coghetti. Of great interest is the marble altar frontal sculpted in relief, originally in the ancient basilica and datable between the end of the XVth and beginning of the XVIth century.

The last chapel is dedicated to Saint Benedict, founder of monasticism in the West and of the oldest monastic order. The statue of the sainted abbot holding the book of his monastic Rule, the fundamental text which inspired many founders of religious orders, is the work of Pietro Tenerani (1789-1869).

This chapel, too, is by Luigi Poletti, and was built between 1843 and 1845.

The architect here makes clear reference to the architecture of classical antiquity, creating a space recalling ancient thermal baths, distinguished by harmony and elegance, although somewhat cold as was typical of Poletti's work. The faceted precious marble columns with capitals representing stylized leaves and flowers, found during excavations at the beginning of the XIXth century in the area of Veio near Isola Farnese, were given to Poletti by Pope Gregory XVI to be used in construction of the chapel.

The Monastery and Cloister

The first testimony of a monastic building at the service of the basilica is contained in a written text of 604 by Pope Gregory the Great. He speaks of two distinct communities at San Paolo: one of nuns devoted to Saint Stephen, and a male community whose protector was Saint Cesarius, martyr of Terracina.

However, precise information about the two religious houses is missing until around the first half of the VIIIth century, when in the *Liber Pontificalis* Pope Gregory II asks the abbot of San Cesario to found one unified community, since the other house was by that time extinct for lack of religious vocations.

From the architectural viewpoint, the building has no particularly distinguishing features; it was a monastery and as such the site of a community which also externally had to witness to the virtue of poverty. Today, with the exception of the cloister, little remains of the ancient monastery, used in the IXth century also as a place of defense of the basilica against barbarian raids from the sea. Adjoining the south transept, the cloister without doubt represents the most beautiful and meaningful witness to the early monastic space.

The inscription along the architrave tells us that construction was begun on a commission from

Cardinal Pietro di Capua from Amalfi, and brought to its conclusion by the abbot of San Paolo, Giovanni Caetani di Andrea, between 1212 and 1235. Of the four sides, the only one attributable with certainty is the north one, assignable to the workshop of the Vassalletto family, well-known Roman sculptors. It is distinguished by a skillful decoration revealing a very high cultural level on the part of its authors, who drew from both classical and Oriental and Etruscan figurative repertories.

Inside the cloister is a statue of *Pope Boniface IX*, seated on a throne with his hand raised in blessing. The statue's origin is unknown; it has particular historical value for the work promoted by the pope in favor of the basilica between the end of the XIVth and beginning of the XVth centuries.

Statue of *Pope Boniface IX. Cloister of the basilica*

The Belltower

The visit to San Paolo fuori le Mura ends with the belltower, which looms over the church with its 65 meters of height. It too is the work of the architect Poletti, whose rich and complex personality it reflects.

The current belltower is divided into five levels characterized by the overlapping of various geometric forms, and is faced with travertine slabs. The belfry contains seven bronzes, four of them from the ancient basilica.

The original XIVth century belltower was demolished, even though it was not damaged in the fire, a fact that provoked polemical and contrasting opinions. Today, objectively speaking, it does not seem to be a particularly distinguished work.

Within the context of pilgrimages, intrinsic to the Roman basilicas, it is nonetheless important that each of them have some structural referent visible and identifiable also at a distance. The dome of Saint Peter's certainly fills this need, just as the great obelisk of San Giovanni in Laterano indicates the presence of the cathedral of Rome also from very far away; San Paolo's belltower guides the steps of those who wish to venerate the tomb of the Apostle, while Santa Maria Maggiore, built on a hill, at least in ancient times rose high above the houses surrounding it.

On facing page, the ancient cloister of San Paolo fuori le Mura, realized in part by the workshop of the Vassalletto family

The belltower rebuilt in the nineteenth century by the architect Poletti

SANTA MARIA MAGGIORE

A Story between Legend and Reality

Pages 120-121, Jacopo Torriti, *The Coronation of the Virgin*, detail of the apse mosaics

Masolino, *Pope Liberius Founding the Basilica of Saint Mary of the Snow*, detail. Naples, Museo Nazionale di Capodimonte

The pilgrim who today goes to venerate Mary in the most ancient Christian basilica in the West dedicated to her, will have a hard time feeling the same emotion as the early faithful who, climbing the slopes of the Esquiline hill, the highest in Rome, saw the church separated from the rest of the city and towering above palaces and houses.

The building was certainly not as majestic as it is today, nor as magnificent as the one Constantine willed to be built over Peter's tomb, but it was nonetheless imposing for its size

and, above all, for the idea behind its origin. Differently from what had been the case until then, the initiative to build it did not come from emperors or the powerful, but directly from the people who, urged by the pope reigning during that time, contributed generously to its construction.

The fact that a pope assumed directly the initiative of building a place of worship marks, in the opinion of some historians, the beginning of a distancing of the church from the authority of the emperor, and of a form of political power for the papacy.

But the active participation of the people in the construction of the church reveals also the love of all for Mary, since the sacred building was dedicated to the Mother of Jesus.

As we did with the other three basilicas, the natural goal of jubilee pilgrimages, we shall visit the church of Santa Maria Maggiore not only with the intention of capturing its history and the aspects of its art, but also of discovering the profound motives that caused it to be built and that, as a precious gift, were handed down to us by preceding generations.

The earliest notice we have of a place of worship in Rome dedicated to the Virgin is in the *Liber Pontificalis*, which tells of a church that Pope Liberius (352-366) had built next to "Livia's market." This note led to the belief that the current basilica, originally commissioned by Sixtus III (432-440), was erected on the ruins of the first one. This hypothesis has been placed in discussion by recent excavations, which have revealed the existence under the basilica of a complex of Roman buildings from imperial times. Today, in light of these discoveries, it is possible to think that if a church dedicated to

Mosaics on the
loggia of the facade
representing
*The Virgin
Announcing the
Miracle to John,
John the Patrician
Before Pope
Liberius, Christ
Enthroned*

Mary existed, it could have been nearby, but was not on the same site as the current one.

This hypothetical building, in any case, was called "Liberian" after the pope's name of Liberius, and this title was extended, obviously only in an ideal sense, to the present basilica.

The story of the construction of the first church has legendary origins and is highly evocative. It is narrated to us by one Fra Bartolomeo da Trento in the XIIIth century. He tells of a rich and pious senator named Giovanni Patricio (John the Patrician) and his wife who, unable to have children, decided to destine to the church their goods and property. In the night of the

Looking through the great arches of the upper loggia on the facade of the current church one can see this legend portrayed in mosaic.

Still today, on 5 August, is celebrated the liturgical feast of the Virgin called the "*Madonna of the Snow*" (numerous churches throughout the world are dedicated to her); on this feastday, during celebration of Mass at the high altar of the basilica in Rome, white jasmine and rose petals are showered down.

But there is an even more unusual fact. In the great nave of the basilica, under a circular slab of granite, it is thought that the senator Giovanni Patricio and his wife are buried, brought here from the nearby baptistry by Pius IX (1846-1878).

In a note of 22 February 1746, during the reign of Benedict XIV (1740-1758), it says that an examination of a sepulchre indicated as that of "John the Patrician" revealed male and female bones with small vases of perfumes and scraps of cloth. The information is certainly interesting, to say the least, but does not prove that the relics are really those of the presumed cofounder of the basilica.

In Santa Maria Maggiore, truly, reality and legend are melded, not to force history beyond the bounds of legitimacy, but to give tangible form to a profound affection, one with which all the ages have surrounded the gentle image of the Mother of God.

Stefano di Giovanni, called Sassetta, *The Virgin of the Snow*, detail of the predella representing *The Construction of Santa Maria Maggiore*. Florence, Galleria degli Uffizi, Contini Bonacossi collection

Nonae of August (between the 4th and 5th of the month) of the year 358, the Virgin Mary appeared in a dream both to Giovanni Patricio and to Pope Liberius, asking that a basilica be dedicated to her on a site in Rome where, that night, it would snow. The next morning the rich senator and the pope went to the Cispian, where in that very night a heavy snow had fallen. Here Liberius, watched by a great crowd of the faithful, traced the outline of the future church in the fresh snow, following the custom of ancient architects who, before starting to build, would sketch out the design of the building on the ground, to actual size.

Construction of the Basilica

L ooking at it objectively, the area designated for the construction of the new basilica was not the most suitable; the terrain was particularly uneven, and the zone was already densely built up.

Thus it is easy to imagine that the reason for such a decision was more ideological than practical. The choice of the highest hill ensured that

The Council of Ephesus and Its Historical Context

The basilica of Santa Maria Maggiore as it appears today owes its true beginnings to one event and one man.

The event is the Ecumenical Council at Ephesus in 431, when Mary was officially declared the Mother of God. The man is Sixtus III, the pope who a few years after that declaration determined that a church dedicated to the Virgin be built on the Esquiline hill.

The heretical controversies that in the IVth century had divided the Christian communities of the largest city in the empire and had been the source of tumult and episodes of intolerance, did not end with the end of the century.

A particularly heartfelt problem was the role of women within the Christian community, linked to the importance attributed to the Virgin Mary in the divine plan for Salvation. In the West, where the pagan world had already assigned to women a role in worship, and where the very existence of Christian communities owed a great deal to female figures like the empress Helen, mother of the emperor Constantine, the Virgin was already the object of devotion. In the East, where the heritage of the Hebrew tradition was stronger, many communities adhered to the schism whose spokesman was the patriarch of Constantinople Nestorius, who asserted that Christ had two distinct natures, human and divine, and consequently that Mary was only the mother of the man Jesus and not the Mother of God. Cyril of Alexandria and Pope Celestine I (422-432) opposed this heresy, condemning Nestorius in a synod held in Rome in 430.

Starting at the beginning of the Vth century the Western imperial authority progressively declined in favor of the court of Constantinople. From 425, the government of the West was in the hands of Galla Placidia, to whom the Eastern emperor Theodosius II had entrusted the regency, as his son Valentinian III was still too young. When the patriarch Nestorius appealed to the emperor in Constantinople, Theodosius II, to obtain sanction from a council, Valentinian III had no choice but to support his position, isolating in this way the Church of Rome.

The council opened at Ephesus in June 431. The choice of this site was practically obligatory, because according to tradition the Virgin had spent the last years of her life in that city.

The session began before the legates from Rome and the bishops from the patriarchate of Antioch had arrived.

Nestorius was cited to appear before the council, but refused and was condemned. A few days later, the bishops from Antioch arrived, but refused to subscribe to the decrees of condemnation, excommunicating Cyril of Alexandria who was presiding over the council.

In the meantime also the papal legate, the deacon Sixtus, had reached Ephesus; reading over the minutes of the session's proceedings, he brought to bear the growing weight that the church of Rome was acquiring because of its apostolic origins, its antiquity and charisma. The Nestorian heresy was condemned, and the Virgin officially awarded the title of "Mother of God" (*Theokotos*).

Polychrome glass, mid-Vth century, *The Cross of Galla Placidia*, detail. Brescia, Museo Civico di Santa Giulia

The Pope of the Basilica of Santa Maria Maggiore: Sixtus III

Sixtus III (432-440) was born in Rome, but we know little else about his youth and training.

Saint Augustine mentions him in a letter concerning a certain amount of sympathy for the Pelagian heresy, which he quickly overcame. On 31 July 432, just four days after the death of his predecessor Saint Celestine (422-432), he was elected pope and set to work immediately to unite the Eastern church. In this he was aided also by the emperor Theodosius II. In the spring of 433, the bishop Saint Cyril and the bishops of the patriarchate of Antioch, presided by John, signed the "Act of Union," and John himself in a letter to the pope recognized the latter's primacy over all the Church.

In Rome the pope was very active in the beautification of the city and religious buildings. He transformed the church of San Lorenzo in Lucina into a basilica with a nave and two aisles, the Lateran baptistry from circular into octagonal, and erected the church of San Pietro in Vincoli.

His most imposing and majestic work was, however, the basilica of Santa Maria Maggiore, destined to glorify Mary's divine maternity.

Pope Sixtus III died on 19 August 440 and was buried near the tomb of Saint Lawrence on the Via Tiburtina.

the church would emerge above the others. The Council of Ephesus had represented a victory for the Church of Rome over the Arian and Nestorian heresies, and the church, built immediately after that council, had to act as the symbol and bulwark of orthodoxy against every form of heresy.

All the buildings standing on the site were torn down, and the rubble, mixed with dirt, was used to level the ground.

On this newly obtained space, construction began of the basilica, using, it seems, the same workmen who had until thirty years before been building for the emperor the church of San Paolo on the Via Ostiense. It is said that all the work on the church, from the foundations to the decoration and consecration, was completed during the nine years of Sixtus III's papacy, but this, given the complexity of the task, does not seem credible. Scholars today tend to think that in reality work began some years earlier, before Sixtus became pope, and that he accelerated it and brought it to its definitive conclusion.

Once the structure was done, the basilica appeared as a typical Early Christian church, with the nave marked off from the two side aisles by two rows of 20 columns each. It measured 86.54 meters long and 32.5 meters wide. The trussed roof and the windows of the nave, twice as many as in the current church, would certainly have made the entire space seem very light both in the sense of weight and luminosity.

The apse, which has since been reconstructed, had five windows; in the center of the vault was an image of the Madonna and Child.

The Church as It Appears Today

Next to the Early Christian basilica built by Sixtus III have been added other elements over the centuries: an elegant bell-tower that rises to a height of 75 meters, some chapels, and an apse realized by Carlo Rinaldi (1611-1691), modifying an earlier design by Gian Lorenzo Bernini, the great architect of the colonnade at Saint Peter's, who was buried here in Santa Maria Maggiore.

The most characteristic architectural element of the church is its facade, inserted between two matching smaller buildings built between 1605 and 1735, at a distance of more than a century from each other. This is the work of the Florentine Ferdinando Fuga (1699-1781), author also of the overall restoration of the interior.

The facade is articulated in two registers: the lower one, as it appears still today, is made up of a portico with five openings, and above it is the large triple-arched Benediction Loggia.

It is to Fuga's credit that he saved the early medieval mosaic that was on the church's original facade. Heavily restored, the mosaic represents the legend of Pope Liberius and John the Patrician.

The basilica of Santa Maria Maggiore

The Baroque
facade of Santa
Maria Maggiore.
On the right, in
the center of the
square, is the
marble column
from the early
basilica of
Massentius

View of the apse
with in the
foreground the
ancient obelisk
brought here by
Pope Sixtus V

An Architect and a Pope, the New Fathers of the Current Basilica

In chapter documents dated August 1740 in the Liberian archives, we read: "The basilica's porch is falling down, held up by panels... the stairs behind the tribune are disconnected because of the shaky terrain... the floor is in bad condition, and what is most urgent, the roofs leak rainwater onto the ceilings, and not only are they in need of restoration, but even more their drainpipes." This dramatic report was presented to the newly elected pope: the archbishop of Bologna, Prospero Lambertini, who took the name of Benedict XIV (1740-1758). The sum of 20,000 *scudi* was immediately appropriated for the rescue operation. Ferdinando Fuga was entrusted with the project; in January 1741 work began to demolish the old porch. On 4 March the first stone was laid of the new building. At the same time also the interior of the basilica became a sort of construction site, with the goal of a general restoration. At the end of 1742 work on the loggia was concluded, and on 15 August 1743 the pope gave his blessing from it.

Von Pastor, in his history of the Papes from the late Middle Ages to the XXth century, early reports heavy criticism expressed by Benedict XIV of the radical transformation worked especially on the apse arch: "We have no reason to boast too much about this work, someone could think that we are theatre impresarios, since it looks like a ballroom."

His negative judgment is completely contradicted by this same pope in private correspondence, when he says "the renovations and embellishment that we effected in that basilica" were "all a great success."

In reality, Fuga had attempted a compromise between the need to maintain the ancient proportions of the basilica and to harmonize, giving a modern shape to the whole, the countless stratifications that had accumulated over the centuries.

Giuseppe Maria Crespi, *Benedict XIV*. Vatican, Picture Gallery

The Interior of the Basilica

The modern pilgrim entering Santa Maria Maggiore today will find it difficult, if not impossible, to relate what he sees to the original Early Christian basilica.

And yet, the space is the same as that of the ancient church; ancient too, even though restored and reworked, are the mosaics placed on the side walls and on the facade of the apse. The exuberant majesty typical of the XVIIth century overlays and obliterates the sober style of the Early Christian basilica. It will thus be our concern to observe the church more in its details than in its overall effect. Our guiding idea will be not to separate the parts from the whole, but more simply to let every aspect express itself according to the specific nature of the epoch when it was made and the artist who created it.

The interior of the basilica looking toward the baldacchino

The Floor and Wooden Ceiling

Upon entering, the eye of the visitor is immediately struck by the richness and beauty of the floor and the wooden ceiling. The Cosmati-work floor, even though restored numerous times, is largely the original made in the XIIth century under Pope Eugene III (1145-1153). Two Romans of noble birth, Giovanni and Scoto Paparoni, had offered a significant sum of money for its creation. During the restoration directed by the architect Fuga in the XVIIIth century, a mosaic panel was lost which it was said represented the two men on horseback.

The coffered wooden ceiling, a later addition, was designed by Leon Battista Alberti (1406-1472) and completed by Antonio da Sangallo the Elder (c. 1455-1534), the brother of Giuliano (c. 1445-1516) who had worked on it before him.

This was the epoch of Alexander VI (1492-1503) and Christopher Columbus, the time of great voyages of exploration and the conquest of new territories. The pope's coat-of-arms inside a garland is a prominent feature of the central row of sunken panels, along with that of Callistus III (1455-1458), the pope who promoted the construction of the ceiling. A tradition, which is not supported by documentation, says that the gold used to decorate the wooden ceiling was donated by Queen Isabel of Castille (1451-1504) and was part of the treasure Columbus brought back with him from his first trip to the Americas. This is unlikely, as it is known that he brought back very few precious objects from his first voyage.

In any case, the impression one receives looking at the ceiling is worthy of Alberti's words as he prepared to design it: "My wish is that in the church there be so much beauty, that nothing greater can be imagined, in any other place." The Romans, summing up the splendor of the ceiling and the gold of the mosaics could exclaim, "Santa Maria Maggiore is all of gold," a popular saying still today.

View of the north aisle

On facing page, the rich inlaid ceiling designed by Antonio da Sangallo the Elder

The Chapels

Along the walls of the two side aisles are chapels, the best known of which, the Sistine and the Pauline, face each other to the right and left of the high altar.

The chapels, all built at a later time than the original church, became over the centuries the designated site for funerary monuments of popes and cardinals who had been directly connected with the basilica and wanted to continue this connection in an ideal sense even after their death.

The first chapel, opening onto the right aisle, was originally called the "chapel of the winter choir;" here the canons of the basilica would meet to pray and to sing the psalms of the liturgy of the Hours.

In 1605 it was transformed into a baptistry by Flaminio Ponzio (1559/60-1613). In 1825 it was reworked further by Giuseppe Valadier (1762-1839), who added the red porphyry basin, giving it the aspect it has today.

Particularly worthy of note is the high relief on the altar representing *The Assumption of the Virgin*, by Pietro Bernini (1562-1629), father of the better known Gian Lorenzo. These two artists and other members of their family are buried in the basilica in the crypt of the

Below, interior of the main chapel; on the right, the former "Chapel of the Winter Choir" later transformed into the baptistry

Borghese Chapel. A marble slab in the floor records, with a simplicity enriched by the hope awarded by faith, that "together, here, they await the Resurrection."

The Sistine Chapel

Von Pastor writes that the Sistine Chapel, named for Pope Sixtus V (1585-1590), whose decision it was to build it, awarding the commission to Domenico Fontana (1563-1607), was envisioned "in such proportions that it seemed a large new church." In its construction were used marble and other stones taken in part from ancient Roman monuments and in part recovered from the old Lateran Palace, at the time in ruins, which Sixtus V in his active restoration campaign returned to its ancient splendor.

The chapel is on a Greek cross plan, faced with marble and topped by a dome decorated with Mannerist paintings by a group of artists, directed by the best known of them, Cesare Nebbia (c. 1536-1614). In the center of the Sistine Chapel, on the altar four angels hold an elegant ciborium in the form of a *tempietto*, a distinguished example of the goldsmith's art designed by Giovan Battista Ricci (1537-1627), which repeats the model of the chapel itself.

In the walls on either side of the ciborium are funerary monuments to Sixtus V and Pius V (1566-72), his predecessor who had managed to stop the Turkish advance on 7 October 1571 with the victory of Lepanto, and for this feat considered a great and valiant defender of the faith. The body of Pius V

On facing page, view of the Sistine Chapel

Arnolfo di Cambio, *Crèche*, detail of *Saint Joseph, the Ox and the Ass.* Crypt of the Sistine Chapel

was transferred to Santa Maria Maggiore from Saint Peter's on 9 January 1588. After his beatification in 1672, his mortal remains were placed in the sarcophagus under his statue, as it appears today.

In honor of the two popes, who belonged to the Dominican and Franciscan orders respectively, in niches to the sides of the two monuments are on one side statues of *Saint Dominic* and *Saint Peter Martyr*, and on the other *Saint Francis of Assisi* and *Saint Anthony of Padua*.

Sixtus V himself inaugurated his monument on 30 July 1589, and a year later, at his death, was buried in the chapel crypt.

The Sistine Chapel, however, conceals a much greater treasure than its statues, frescoes, and marbles. This is the Crypt of the Crèche, reached by a staircase in front of the altar.

This crypt, located under the altar of the Sistine Chapel, although not in the geographic center of the basilica is nonetheless its heart. Here are preserved as relics some of the boards said to have been part of the cradle of Jesus, sent to Rome, it seems, during the papacy of Theodore I (642-649).

Pope Nicholas IV (1288-1292) created the project of building a Nativity scene as a chapel designed to give renewed emphasis to the relics of the manger. Arnolfo di Cambio (c. 1245-1302) was given the commission of realizing both the architecture and the statuary, but little remains today of his work, since the small oratory was actually moved in 1590 by Fontana during construction of the current Sistine Chapel.

From a series of illustrations and a report made directly by the architect, an expert in complex transports like that of the obelisk in Saint Peter's Square, we know that by using a system of pulleys and winches suspended from the vault of the new structure, Fontana enclosed the entire Chapel of the Crèche, detached from its foundations, in a sturdy wooden framework and set it down in the center of the new edifice below the level of the floor, to create its crypt. The

On facing page, the dome of the Sistine Chapel; below, the dome of the Pauline Chapel

operation was praised as a perfect success, but the structure probably suffered some damage. Today it is possible to admire *in loco* some of Arnolfo's statues, but the group of the Virgin and Child has been lost, substituted by a XVIth century *Virgin Enthroned* attributed to Pietro Paolo Olivieri.

The Pauline Chapel

At the end of the left aisle, right across from the Sistine Chapel, is the Pauline Chapel, which seems a twin to the other even though it was inaugurated about 25 years later. Built by Flaminio Ponzio (1559/60-1613) for Paul V (1605-1621) of the Borghese family, it too is on a Greek cross plan, covered by a dome and faced with extravagant marble decorations. It can by rights be considered the Chapel of the Virgin, as it holds on the altar an ancient and

The Icon of the Madonna "Salus Populi Romani"

The altar of the Pauline Chapel with icon of the Virgin

A very old legend recounts that Saint Luke the Evangelist was a painter, and that among the images he painted was a portrait of the Virgin Mary. Many artists have portrayed the saint intent on painting the sweet face of the Mother of God. The legend very likely arose from the fact that Luke, among the Evangelists, is the one who narrates most fully the birth of Jesus and in this context speaks at length about the Mother of the Savior, to the point that he is traditionally indicated simply as Mary's biographer.

A number of icons are attributed to him: in Italy, for example, in Bologna a famous Marian sanctuary is dedicated to the Madonna of Saint Luke.

The Madonna in the basilica of Santa Maria Maggiore is also a "Virgin by Saint Luke."

In reality all of Saint Luke's icons were painted during the Middle Ages.

The history of the basilica includes the story of an image of the Virgin donated by Pope Paschal I (817-824). During the papacy of Leo IV (847-855) a violent fire destroyed the Vatican neighborhood called the Borgo. This image of the Virgin was carried in procession and the fire died out; even earlier occurs the story of another procession with the image of the Virgin ordered by Saint Gregory the Great (590-604) to cause a grave attack of the plague to cease. These are just a few episodes which underline the intimate relationship of faith and devotion between the Romans and the image in Santa Maria Maggiore, invoked often as the "Salvation of the Roman people." None of this, however, authorizes us to think that the image referred to in these stories is the one venerated today on the altar of the Borghese Chapel; but even though it is impossible to establish the date of its execution and its author, nonetheless its link between the faithful and the Mother of God remains a valid reality. Pius XII (1939-1958) crowned her on 1 November 1954 in Saint Peter's Square, in the presence of an immense crowd, confirming in this way what generations of history had always affirmed.

precious icon to which the Roman people have been devoted for numerous centuries, invoked by the name of *Salus populi romani* (Salvation of the Roman people).

Confirmation of the destination of the chapel to the veneration of Mary is provided by a marble bas-relief by Stefano Maderno (1576-1636), high above the altar, representing Pope Liberius intent on tracing in the snow the outline of the first church of Santa Maria Maggiore.

On facing page, view of the Pauline Chapel

To the sides, funerary monuments to Clement VIII and Paul V, designed by Flaminio Ponzio, were realized in imitation of the two monuments in the Sistine Chapel.

Numerous artists from the same period, such as for example the Cavalier D'Arpino (1568-1640), author of the lunette above the altar and the pendentives of the dome, and Guido Reni (1575-1642), who painted the vaults, contributed to the embellishment of this space, which in opulence and splendor was meant to exceed every other decoration of the basilica's interior.

Paul V himself ordered that no expense be spared in the materials used (we even know the

total sum spent on the chapel, truly astronomical for that time: 299,261 *scudi* and 61 *baiocchi*), and the sumptuousness and magnificence of the whole should be seen as a contribution of faith and love to the one who was being celebrated as the Mother of God.

A detail that perhaps not everyone knows: Paolina Bonaparte, sister of the emperor Napoleon, who after the death of her first husband married Camillo Borghese, is buried in the crypt of the chapel.

Two views of the imposing baldacchino by Fuga with the apse mosaics in the background

The Apse of the Church

The new apse of the basilica, replacing the original one built during the papacy of Sixtus III, was constructed by Pope Nicholas IV, who enriched it with new mosaics executed by Jacopo Torriti in 1295 and frescoes of the school of Cavallini. However, many more centuries still were to pass before the space took on its current appearance.

Pope Benedict XIV offered his contribution to the major work of renovation of the interior in preparation for the jubilee of 1750, remodeling the altar with the red porphyry sarcophagus which according to tradition held the remains of Giovanni Patricio and his wife. Above it, he had Fuga build the great porphyry and bronze *baldacchino*, which turned out, however, to be somewhat too large, obscuring the view of the mosaics in the apse vault.

In the following century, Pius IX (1846-1878) - who on 8 December 1854 had proclaimed the dogma of the Immaculate Conception of Mary - had the crypt under the altar of the Confession remodeled. The richness of the different colors of marble used was to serve, the pope intended, to honor the relics of the manger, contained in a precious crystal urn in the shape of a cradle sustained by angels.

A statue of Pius IX at prayer, a fairly mediocre work by the sculptor Ignazio Iacometti, was placed by Leo III in the crypt in memory of the pope who had honored with filial devotion the Mother of God.

HIERVSALE

The Mosaics and Their Meaning

The most interesting aspect of the entire basilica is without doubt the mosaics. They are the living witness to the original church. Their theological and biblical value is enhanced by the customs of that time which favored the use of images, immediately understandable to all, to narrate the story of Salvation even to those who could not read. It is true that missing from the original mosaics of the period of Sixtus III are those that were in the apse, substituted by the current ones of a much later epoch, but above and beyond the difference in style we can presume that it was the Virgin with the Child in her arms that took center place in the old apse as well, so that the unified iconographical program with its Marian and Christological content remains the same.

To all this must be added the problem of the

restoration of images which deteriorated over time, the repainting in fresco of ruined mosaics, the destruction of entire frames (three per side) at the time the Sistine Chapel and later the Pauline Chapel were opened.

In the nave, only 27 of the original 42 mosaics remain, although it is possible to identify the contents of the 6 destroyed frames from some XVIIth century drawings.

A thematic examination of the mosaics starts from the ones under the windows in the nave, originally 42, from the left looking at the altar, beginning with the last frame next to the triumphal arch. On these two walls the entire history of the Old Testament is narrated through its most significant figures. On the left Abraham, Isaac, and Jacob are links in the chain that from generation to generation leads to the birth of the Messiah. On the right, with Moses and Joshua and the long forty-year march through the desert which led the Hebrew people from slavery in Egypt to the Promised Land, we can read

The mosaics on the triumphal arch, and (facing page) detail of *The Heavenly Jerusalem*

Apse mosaics by
Jacopo Torriti
with *The
Coronation of the
Virgin*, and below,
*Scenes from the
Life of the Virgin*

a foreshadowing of the radical liberation of man which the Savior would bring about with his birth, death, and resurrection.

The promises made in the Old Testament are fulfilled in the person of Jesus, the Son of God made man, born of the Virgin Mary. This theme is described in the mosaics on the triumphal arch.

All the scenes refer to the infancy of Jesus, as described in the Gospels of Luke (chapters 1-2) and Matthew (chapters 1-2), and are arranged in three registers, one above the other, each divided into two sections. *The Angel's Annunciation to Mary, The Revelation to Joseph of the Virginal Conception of his Betrothed*, and *The Adoration of the Magi* are some of the episodes il-

lustrated. Below, the cities of Bethlehem and Jerusalem represent the synthesis of the whole story of Salvation: Bethlehem the city of David, the king from whose descendants the Messiah would be born, marks the last story from the Old Testament; Jerusalem, the city of the death and resurrection of Jesus Christ, is the starting point of a new path for mankind.

The twelve sheep, six on each side, looking out of the gates of the two cities are clearly the symbol of this new people of God, who, guided by Jesus the Good Shepherd, set out on the path to Salvation.

At the center of the triumphal arch is shown the Cross above a throne, the final symbol of the Salvation offered by Christ and witnessed by

Jacopo Torriti, *Nativity*; on facing page, detail of the mosaic decorations of the apse

Pages 152-153, detail of the apse mosaic representing a river god and a ship

Mosaics in the nave: *Moses and Pharaoh's Daughters*, detail; right, *The Conquest of Jericho*, detail

the Church, represented by the Apostles Peter and Paul at the sides of the throne.

The vault of the apse, as said above, is not the original one; these mosaics were realized between 1291 and 1296 by Jacopo Torriti.

At a distance of centuries, the thematic discourse enunciated in the early mosaics does not lose its value, rather it is confirmed and enhanced, emphasizing the fact that the promise of the Old Testament which is fulfilled in the New finds in Mary its culmination and synthesis.

The apse is divided into two distinct sectors: in the vault is the scene of *The Coronation of the Virgin*, and below, in the band running between the windows, are scenes from the life of the Virgin. At the center of this band is the *Dormitio Virginis*, a term used traditionally to underline Mary's simple passage from this life to the next. There seems to be no indication of the Assumption; however, it is confirmed explicitly in the upper section of the mosaic, both in the glorification of Mary and in the inscription at the foot of the throne, which says "The Virgin Mary assumed into the dwelling place of the heavens, where the King of Kings sits on the starry

Mosaics in the nave: *Abraham and Lot*; **on facing page,** *The Hospitality of Abraham*

Page 158, *Crossing the Red Sea*

throne. The Holy Mother of God is elevated into the Kingdom of Heaven, above choirs of angels."

The words in the open book in Christ's left hand give the meaning of the entire picture: "Come my beloved and I will place you on my throne." Not two thrones, but one, to underline the intimate relationship uniting the Mother and Son in the plan for the redemption of mankind.

The church, represented by the saints that sur-round Jesus Christ and the Virgin, in her glori-fication recognizes in advance the final destiny of all mankind.

This image and the meanings it manifests are a synthesis of the entire history of the basilica of Santa Maria Maggiore. The many interventions and the different sensibilities which have laid layer upon layer over the course of the centuries thus become articulate manifestations of a loving devotion to the one who is the Mother of all.

Essential Bibliography

M. Armellini, *Le chiese di Roma dal secolo IV al XIX*, Rome 1942

P. Brezzi, *La storia degli anni santi*, Milan 1973

Il Vaticano e Roma Cristiana, Rome 1975

A. Carpiceci, *La Fabbrica di San Pietro*, Vatican City, 1983

R. Stopani, *Le grandi vie dei pellegrinaggi del Medioevo*, 1986

R. Luciani (ed. by), *Santa Maria Maggiore e Roma*, Rome 1987

C. Pietrangeli (ed. by), *San Paolo fuori le Mura*, Florence 1989

C. Pietrangeli (ed. by), *La Basilica di San Pietro*, Florence 1990

C. Pietrangeli (ed. by), *San Giovanni in Laterano*, Florence 1991

N. del Re (ed. by), *Mondo Vaticano*, Vatican City 1995

B. Mondin, *Dizionario enciclopedico dei papi*, 1995

G. Rocchi (ed. by), *San Pietro. Arte e storia della Basilica Vaticana*, 1996

© 1999 SCALA Group S.p.A., Antella (Florence)
All rights reserved

Layout: Matilde Contri
Photographs: SCALA ARCHIVE except pp. 62-63, 73, 74, 76, 157, 158
(A. Jemolo, Rome); pp. 64, 72, 75, 77, 79, 87, 94, 106-107, 109, 111,
113, 117, 133, 137, 138, 139, 140, 141, 142, 143, 145 (Vasari, Rome)
Translation: Susan Scott
Editing: Patrizia Bevilacqua

Printed by "Arti Grafiche" StampArte,
Calenzano (Florence), 2005